Michigan

OFF THE BEATEN PATH™

Now that you have all this time on your ... Robt Sheila

"DuFresne does a fine job offering options for every kind of taste, from art lovers to afficionados of the great outdoors."
 —*Grand Rapids Magazine*

"Hit the country roads and explore the hidden gems that DuFresne has discovered."
 —*The Saginaw News*

"This book will come in handy whether you're on a full-scale vacation in Wolverine land or just planning a nice, long Sunday drive."
 —*The Flint Journal*

OFF THE BEATEN PATH SERIES

Michigan

OFF THE BEATEN PATH™

FOURTH EDITION

JIM DuFRESNE

A Voyager Book

Old Saybrook, Connecticut

Illustrations on pages 5, 18, 25, 47, 51, 59, 66, 88, 97, 110, 118, 133, 142, and 156 by Steve Baldwin
Illustrations on pages 43, 72, and 164 by Carole Drong

Library of Congress Cataloging-in-Publication Data
DuFresne, Jim.
   Michigan : off the beaten path / Jim DuFresne. — 4th ed.
      p. cm. — (Off the beaten path series)
   "A voyager book."
   Includes index.
   ISBN 1-56440-886-8
   1. Michigan—Guidebooks. I. Title. II. Series.
F564.3.D84 1996
917.7404'43—dc20   95-26441
                                                              CIP

Manufactured in the United States of America
Fourth Edition/Second Printing

*To that wonderfully warm and
huggable person I call Mom*

MICHIGAN

WESTERN
UPPER PENINSULA

EASTERN
UPPER PENINSULA

NORTHWEST
MICHIGAN

LAKE
HURON

LAKE
MICHIGAN

THE
THUMB

THE
HEARTLAND

SOUTHEAST
MICHIGAN

CONTENTS

INTRODUCTION

Look at a map of the United States, spin a globe of the world, and the most prominent state is Michigan. It always stands out, regardless of the size of the map or how obscured the detail.

Michigan is set off from the rest of the country by water. Four of the five Great Lakes surround it and have turned most of its borders into 3,200 miles of lakeshore where you sit in the sand and look out on the watery horizon of the world's largest freshwater seas.

Michigan is inundated by water. It's not only outlined by blue, but its history was shaped by the Great Lakes, and today travelers search the state over for a bit of their own sand and surf. In Michigan, there is no short supply. Stand anywhere in the state and you are no more than 85 miles from the Great Lakes and only 6 miles from one of the 11,000 sparkling inland lakes or 36,000 miles of streams and rivers. Come winter, Michigan's water turns fluffy and white and gently lands all around, much to the delight of skiers.

Michigan is water, yet beaches and boating, swimming and sunbathing are only part of the attractions the state has to offer. To the adventurous traveler, to those who love to swing off the interstate highways onto the country roads that wander between the woods and the lakes, there are quaint villages to discover and shipwrecks to explore, art fairs and mushroom festivals to enjoy, wine-tasting tours to savor, a stretch of quiet trail to soothe the urban soul.

All you need is time, a good map of Michigan, and this book. The map can be obtained from the Michigan Travel Bureau by writing (P.O. Box 30226, Lansing 48909) or by calling a toll-free number (800–543–2937). The map will lead you away from the six-lane highways to the scenic country roads and then back again when you are ready to return home.

Michigan: Off the Beaten Path points out those half-hidden gems that travelers rejoice in discovering, from a lighthouse that has become a country inn to party-fishing boats that allow novice anglers to stalk and catch the Great Lakes' tastiest offering, the yellow perch. Because addresses, phone numbers, and hours of operation can change from summer to summer, in the appendix there is a list of regional tourist associations that can provide the most up-to-date information.

Introduction

The same holds true for prices. Inflation, with its annual increases in everything from room rates and restaurant prices to entry fees into parks and museums, will quickly outdate anything listed. Therefore, only the prices for substantial items (rooms, meals, and major attractions) have been provided in this book to help readers judge whether a restaurant or hotel is affordable.

Most of all, more than this book and a map, you need time. Don't shortchange Michigan. Don't try to cover half the state in a weekend holiday. You will only be disappointed at the end of your trip. You could spend a summer exploring Michigan and never leave the shoreline. I have spent a lifetime here, yet my neverending list of places to go and adventures to undertake only grows longer with each journey in the Great Lakes State.

The prices and rates listed in this guidebook were confirmed at press time. We recommend, however, that you call establishments before traveling to obtain current information.

Michigan

OFF THE BEATEN PATH™

SOUTHEAST MICHIGAN

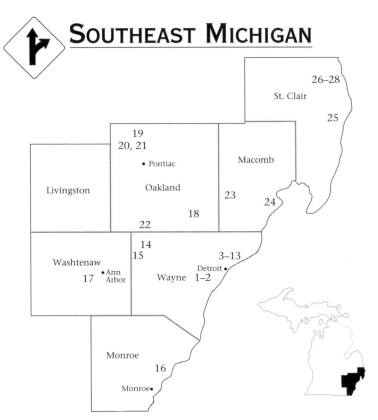

1. Fairlane
2. Ford Wyoming Drive-in
3. Motown Museum
4. Eastern Market
5. R. Hirt Jr. Company
6. Tiger Stadium
7. Lafayette Coney Island
8. People Mover
9. Graystone International Jazz Museum
10. Belle Isle Aquarium
11. Dossin Great Lakes Museum
12. Chene Park
13. Omnimax Theater
14. Maybury State Park
15. Plymouth Historical Museum
16. Monroe County Historical Museum
17. Ann Arbor Hands-On Museum
18. Townsend Hotel
19. Roston Cabin
20. Battle Alley
21. Holly Hotel
22. Star Clipper Train
23. Yates Cider Mill
24. Mount Clemens Train
25. Palmer Park
26. Boat Night
27. The Victorian Inn
28. Port Huron Museum of Arts and History

SOUTHEAST MICHIGAN

Southeast Michigan, a region of seven counties, revolves around metropolitan Detroit, which sprawls into three of them. And Detroit revolves around automobiles. It's as simple as that.

Known best throughout the country as Motor City, Detroit carries several other titles, including Motown, after the recording company that produced such famous singers as Diana Ross and Stevie Wonder before it fled to Los Angeles from its studio on Woodward Avenue. Detroit also has the distinction of being the only city in the United States that lies *north* of the Canadian border. Visitors are surprised when they have to drive south on the Ambassador Bridge to reach Windsor, Ontario.

Detroit and its neighboring suburbs wear many faces; some are good, some are unjustly earned, but the least recognized one is that of a destination for travelers. Detroit is the sixth-largest city in the country, yet despite its size many tourists consider it very much "off the beaten path." Depart from the city and the rest of Southeast Michigan changes quickly, from the urban sprawl to the rolling hills and lakes of northern Oakland County, the blue water of St. Clair and Port Huron, and the culture and carefree college ways of Ann Arbor, the home of the University of Michigan.

WAYNE COUNTY

Until the 1870s, Detroit was a commercial center for farmers, but at the end of that century the first automobiles appeared, as Ransom E. Olds and Henry Ford began tinkering with "horseless carriages." By 1903, Ford had organized the Ford Motor Company, and when he pioneered the assembly-line method of building cars and introduced the Model T, the vehicle for the common man, Detroit's place as the automobile capital of the world was determined.

Cars are a way of life in Detroit. Michigan boasts of having the first mile of concrete rural highway (1909), the first traffic light (1915), and the first urban freeway free of those annoying stoplights (1942). The best-known place to view this history of cars and its immense effect on the American way of life is **Greenfield Village and Henry Ford Museum** (313–271–1620), a 260-acre complex with one hundred historic buildings in Dearborn that has become the nation's largest indoor and outdoor museum.

For a more intimate view of the auto barons themselves, visit one of the many mansions that auto money built and historical societies have since preserved. ❖ **Fairlane,** the Henry Ford estate, is a fifty-six-room mansion located nearby on the University of Michigan–Dearborn campus. Built in 1915 at what was then an astronomical $1.8 million, the home is an extension of Ford's ingenuity wrapped up in his love for functionalism. It often hosted such dignitaries as Thomas Edison, President Herbert Hoover, and Charles Lindbergh. Tours begin underground among the massive turbines and generators that were designed by Ford and his friend Edison in the six-level powerhouse that made the estate self-sufficient in power, heat, light, even ice.

From the outside the house looks modest compared to other historic mansions. But inside you'll find such luxuries as a central vacuum cleaner, a sixty-five-extension phone system, a one-lane bowling alley, and a pool that has been covered and turned into a delightful restaurant that serves lunch. Guided tours lead you through the house and underground tunnels, show you where Edison used to sleep, and tell of April 7, 1947, when the Rogue River flooded and knocked out the powerhouse. That night, without heat, light, or phone service, Ford suffered a cerebral hemorrhage and died by candlelight.

To reach U of M–Dearborn, head west of Southfield Expressway on Michigan Avenue and then north on Greenfield Road, where signs point the way to the small campus. Guided tours of the national historic landmark are offered year-round on Sunday from 1:00 to 4:30 P.M. From April through September 30, Fairlane (313–593–5590) is also open daily with tours offered on the hour from 10:00 A.M. to 3:00 P.M. There is an admission fee.

Movie stars and fresh air . . . you do remember drive-in theaters, don't you? At ❖ **Ford Wyoming Drive-in** in Dearborn it's hard to forget them. Contrary to the popular belief that drive-ins are cinematic dinosaurs of the Bee-Bop Era, this motorized movieland in the hometown of Henry Ford is still packing them in.

Ford Wyoming is the largest drive-in complex in Michigan and currently has eight theaters here—that's right, eight separate screens, each showing a different movie. On a good weekend there will be more than 2,000 cars and somewhere between 5,000 and 8,000 people watching a film.

Ford Wyoming Drive-in (313–846–6910 or 582–2200) is reached from I–94 by departing from exit 210 and heading north on Wyoming Avenue. Some of the screens are entered from Wyoming Avenue and some from Ford Road.

To most people Detroit is Motor City, but to music lovers it will always be Motown, the birthplace of the famous record company that Berry Gordy, Jr., founded in 1960. Gordy started out with $800 and a small recording studio that was built in the back of his Grand Boulevard home. From Studio A emerged the distinct "Motown Sound" and such performers as Marvin Gaye, the Miracles, Gladys Knight and the Pips, the Supremes, The Jackson 5, and a very talented blind singer named Steveland Morris Hardaway, known now as Stevie Wonder. Eventually the famous HITSVILLE U.S.A. sign was hung on the front of the home and Motown expanded into seven additional houses along the street before setting up its Woodward office.

The company continued recording in Studio A until 1972, when it moved its operation to Los Angeles. What remains today at Hitsville U.S.A. is ✣**Motown Museum,** a state historic site. The museum is two adjoining houses filled with gold record awards, old album covers, publicity photos, and even some old Temptation costumes that are viewed to the beat of Motown hits played continuously in every room. For most visitors the intriguing part is Studio A and its control booth, looking as it did twenty-five years ago, when Motown was a struggling recording company.

Motown Museum (313–875–2264) is located at 2648 West Grand Boulevard, 2 blocks west of the exit off the Lodge Freeway. The Museum is open Monday from noon to 5:00 P.M., Tuesday through Saturday 10:00 A.M. to 5:00 P.M., and Sunday 2:30 to 5:00 P.M. There is a small admission fee.

Although Detroit has its mansions and its auto barons, it is known primarily as a blue-collar town, an assembly-line haven that has made it as ethnically diverse as any city in the country. Detroiters love their heritage, ethnic foods, music, and the traditions of an old way of life. The ethnic pride and the love of traditional foods can best be seen at the ✣**Eastern Market,** a farmer's market that is said to be the largest of its kind in the country. Two halls, one open-air, one enclosed, and both decorated with huge murals on the outside, are the heart of the market. On Tuesdays and Saturdays they overflow with shoppers, farmers, and vendors bartering for the freshest fruit, vegetables, flowers, meats, and cheeses to be found in the city. Everything from the farm is on sale here, from homemade bratwurst to live rabbits, and the market makes for an enjoyable stroll, even if you don't intend to buy anything.

Ringing the market are butcher shops, fish markets, and stores specializing in spices, nuts, and foods imported from around the world. The oldest shop is ◆ **R. Hirt Jr. Company** in a three-story red brick building that overlooks the market stalls. Rudolph Hirt Jr. began his business in 1887 with a stall in the old Detroit Central Market, selling eggs, butter, and cheese from local farms. When land in Cadillac Square became too valuable to be used as a farmer's market, Hirt was one of the first to build a store in the new Eastern Market on land the city set aside in 1892.

The building still stands, and the old wooden cheese locker behind the counter is still used, although a much larger one has since been built on the second floor. The second one was needed because 40 percent of Hirt's business is selling cheese: more than 250 kinds, from well-known Swiss cheese and French brie to the little-known Michigan Raw Milk Pinconning that is made in the Upper Peninsula. The shop also sells imported crackers and cookies, teas, jams, at least thirty kinds of mustards, olive oil, and other gastronomic items, all left stacked in their opened cases to make for leisurely and informal browsing. On the third floor, Hirt sells wicker baskets of all descriptions and sizes. You could purchase a basket on the third floor and then easily fill it with enough mouth-watering items on the first floor for a memorable gourmet dinner in the park.

To reach the Eastern Market, head downtown on I–75 and exit east on Mack Avenue. The market is 2 blocks east of the expressway, near the corner of Mack and Russell avenues. R. Hirt Jr. is open Monday through Friday, 7:00 A.M. to 3:00 P.M., and Saturday, 7:00 A.M. to 2:00 P.M.

Restaurants also reflect the ethnically diverse, hard-working Detroiters who at nightfall put aside their jobs and enjoy themselves immensely with good food served in large portions at very reasonable prices.

Coney Island hot dogs and baseball are a summer tradition in the Motor City. It begins at ◆ **Tiger Stadium,** one of the oldest ballparks in the country and home of Detroit's professional baseball team. Built in 1900 and called Bennett Park, the stadium

R. Hirt Jr. Company

has been remodeled and renamed several times but still retains that old-fashioned atmosphere of summer baseball, where the fans feel like an extension of the game rather than passive observers. There have been attempts recently to either cover the old ballpark or build a modern domed stadium for the team, but Detroiters rise in unison each time such proposals are made and overwhelmingly express their love for the historic structure. The Tigers (313–962–4000) play from April to September, and tickets can usually be purchased at game time at the stadium on the corner of Michigan and Trumbull avenues downtown.

To continue the tradition after the ninth inning, head over to ❖ **Lafayette Coney Island,** Detroit's premier hot dog place. Located where Lafayette and Michigan avenues merge near Kennedy Square downtown, the porcelain white eatery with its male waiters is an institution in Detroit. The fare is Coney dogs (with loads of chopped onions, chili, and mustard), loose burgers (loose hamburger in a hot dog bun), and bean soup served on Formica counters and tables with paper napkins and truck-stop china. Yet arrive at midnight, and you'll see patrons dressed in tuxedos enjoying a late-night hot dog after the symphony seated next to a couple of rabid baseball fans with their team pennant. Lafayette Coney Island (313–964–8198) is open twenty-four hours daily with hot dogs and loose burgers priced at around $2.00.

It may not be "off the beaten path," but Detroit's Central Automated Transit System is definitely above the city streets. Better known as the ❖ **People Mover,** the mass transit project was opened in 1987 after several years of controversial delays and cost overruns. The 2.9-mile elevated track circles the downtown heart of Detroit. Its automated cars stop every three minutes at thirteen stations, each decorated with beautiful mosaics and other artwork. The ride costs only 50 cents and lasts only fourteen minutes, but it gives an excellent overall view of the city from a superb vantage point. The best stretch comes when the cars wind around Cobo Hall and passengers see a panorama of the Detroit River and the skyline of Windsor, the Canadian city to the south. The most popular stop has to be the Greektown Station, where riders pile out and head for Monroe Street for dinner at one of the many Greek restaurants. The People Mover (313–962–RAIL) operates 7:00 A.M.–11:00 P.M. Monday–Thursday, until midnight Friday–Saturday, and until 8:00 P.M. Sunday.

7

Motown move over. Long before there was Stevie Wonder or the Temptations, black musicians were picking up their horns to play on the steamers that in the mid-1800s were making regular runs to the Lake Erie resorts on Put-In-Bay.

By the early 1900s, Paradise Valley had emerged as a major force in the development of jazz talent, and then in 1922, the University of Michigan built the Graystone Ballroom along Woodward Avenue, and Detroit entered its golden era for jazz. Eventually Duke Ellington, Tommy Dorsey, Glen Miller, Jimmie Lunceford, and many others played to capacity crowds before the ballroom was torn down in 1980 by its last owner . . . Motown.

Much of the furnishings that survived can now be seen in a replicated section of the ballroom in the ◆ **Graystone International Jazz Museum** along with posters, musical instruments, album covers, and other jazz memorabilia. In 1995 the museum (313–963–3813) moved to a new location in the Book Tower Building, 12409 Washington Boulevard. Call for its current hours. There is a small admission fee.

The Detroit River, which connects Lake St. Clair with Lake Erie, was the avenue that the city's first residents—the French in 1701—used to arrive in Southeast Michigan. The river remains a focal point of activities for Detroiters, with several parks lining its banks and one—Belle Isle—located in the middle of it.

Reached by a bridge at East Jefferson and Grand Boulevard, the island park features the ◆ **Belle Isle Aquarium** (313–267–7159), which opened to the public in 1904, making it one of the oldest freshwater aquariums in the country. The center features thousands of fish in dozens of large tanks, everything from a school of piranhas and a 4-foot-long alligator gar to common bluegill, bass, and rainbow trout. One of the most popular tanks contains an electric eel, and when they feed this fish, at 10:30 A.M., 12:30 P.M., and 2:30 P.M. daily, it is an electrifying affair. The handlers drop a microphone into the tank so onlookers can hear the fish-made electric charges. The aquarium is open daily 10:00 A.M. to 5:00 P.M. There is a small admission fee.

Almost next door to the aquarium on the island is ◆ **Dossin Great Lakes Museum** (313–267–6440), which traces the sailing history of the Great Lakes in several rooms of displays and hands-on exhibits and a video room. A highlight of the museum is the preserved pilothouse from a Great Lakes freighter, which actually looks out on the Detroit River. The museum is open 10:00 A.M. to 5:30 P.M. Wednesday through Sunday. A small donation is requested at the door.

A little more obscure and closer to downtown on Atwater Street is ❖ **Chene Park,** with its outdoor theater, river walkway, and small pond. The delightful little park is a favorite place to wet a fishing line, enjoy a picnic, or take in one of the concerts, many of them free, that are held there throughout the summer. Call the park (313–877–8078) for dates, times, and prices of the outdoor concerts and other events it sponsors.

For kids, a great destination is the **Detroit Science Center,** home of the ❖ **Omnimax Theater.** Located in the Detroit Cultural Center, which includes the renowned Detroit Institute of Art, the science center was built in 1978, and right from the beginning the Omnimax was the highlight of any visit there. The domed theater was the second one built in the country and is still the only one in Michigan.

The theater projects a 70mm film across a domed ceiling that is 67 feet in diameter. The result is a dramatically clearer and more detailed image, due to your increased peripheral vision from the curved screen. Many consider the Omnimax the finest motion picture system in the world. Films change on a six-month schedule and range in topic from a trip to the Antarctic and the Great Barrier Reef to being on the deck of the *Stars and Stripes* with Dennis Connor in the America's Cup Race.

Regardless of the subject, any film will have you gripping the arm rests of your tilted chair and departing "The Max" amazed and a little wobbly from the visual experience. On the second floor, the science center also has more than fifty hands-on science exhibits.

From I–75 depart at the Warren exit and turn west onto Warren Avenue to reach the center (313–577–8400) in a half mile. Hours are 10:00 A.M. to 2:00 P.M. Monday through Friday and 10:30 A.M. to 6:00 P.M. Saturday and Sunday. There is an admission charge for the center that includes the Omnimax Theater.

In 1975, the Michigan Department of Natural Resources opened ❖ **Maybury State Park** on an existing farm in the northwest corner of Wayne County. It was an unusual place to establish a state park, but Maybury is an unusual state park. The idea was to preserve a "living farm" close to the city so that residents, especially children, who have never experienced the sights, sounds, and yes, smells of a working farm would have the opportunity to do so nearby. The area consists of several barns where visitors get a close, hanging-on-the-fence view of chickens, pigs, cows, goats, sheep, horses, and other typical farm animals. There is also a display of old farming equipment, but newer plows and harvesters are used by the staff who actually work the land. Kids not only get to feed the animals but also can view newborn chicks in the brooder room, modern tractors rumbling along, and huge draft horses pulling a plow through fields of corn, oats, beans, and other typical Michigan crops.

Also within the 1,000-acre state park are natural areas of meadows and forests with hiking trails and bike paths. A park concessionaire runs a horse stable with 8 miles of horse trails that during the winter become the destination for Nordic skiers who can rent equipment at the park. But by far the most unusual aspect of Maybury is its Living Farm, which is open daily from 10:00 A.M. to 7:00 P.M. in the summer and 10:00 A.M. until 5:00 P.M. in the winter. Maybury State Park (810–349–8390) has an entrance on Eight Mile Road, 5 miles west of I–275. A vehicle fee is charged to enter the park.

In 1882 the Plymouth Iron Windmill Company began to manufacture and give away small BB guns to farmers to encourage them to purchase one of its windmills. Within four years, the northwest corner of Wayne County was well "windmilled," but the company kept producing the air rifles. Eventually Plymouth Iron Windmill Company became Daisey Manufacturing Company, and this small town was known as the "air rifle capital of the world" until the operations was moved to Arkansas in 1958.

You could learn about the start of Daisey air rifles and see a collection of the earliest models at the ◆ **Plymouth Historical Museum.** The museum also has many other exhibits, period rooms, and even "downtown Plymouth" in the early 1900s, but it is the display of Daisey air rifles that brings back fond memories of tin cans in the backyard to so many of us.

To reach Plymouth Historical Museum (313–455–8940) from I–275, depart at exit 28, head west on Ann Arbor Road, and then turn north on Main Street. Hours are 1:00 P.M. to 4:00 P.M. Wednesday, Thursday, and Saturday, and 2:00 to 5:00 P.M. Sunday. There is a small admission fee.

MONROE COUNTY

General George Armstrong Custer may have staged his ill-fated "Last Stand" at Little Bighorn in Montana, but he grew up in Monroe, Michigan. Custer was actually born in Rumley, Ohio, but spent most of his youth, until he entered a military academy at the age of sixteen, living with his half sister in this city along Lake Erie. Even after he became a noted brigadier general during the Civil War, Custer continued to return to Monroe, and in 1864 he married Elizabeth Bacon, his boyhood sweetheart, here.

Custer's intriguing life can be traced at the ◈ **Monroe County Historical Museum,** which features the largest collection of the general's personal artifacts in the country. The Custer exhibit room occupies a fourth of the museum floor and focuses on his youth in Monroe and his distinguished Civil War career rather than his well-known days on the western plains. There is an overcoat of buffalo hide that he wore during a winter campaign in 1868 and a buckskin suit that is impressive with its beadwork and porcupine quills. Custer was an avid outdoorsman and also a fine taxidermist. It comes as a surprise to many that Custer enjoyed mounting the game animals he hunted, and housed in the museum along with his favorite Remington buffalo rifle are many mounted game animals.

The museum also has displays on Monroe's early history, which dates back to French missionaries in 1634, and on the famous Battle of River Raisin in 1813. But it is the life and tragic death of General Custer that most people find fascinating. The Monroe County Historical Museum (313–243–7137) is at 126 South Monroe Street in the heart of the city and is open Wednesday through Sunday from 10:00 A.M. to 5:00 P.M. During the summer through September it is open daily. There is a small admission fee.

WASHTENAW COUNTY

Trendy Ann Arbor, the cultural capital of Southeast Michigan (and some say the entire state), is the site of the University of Michigan, the "Harvard of the West." The university dominates the city, its buildings and campus entwined in the town's landscape. It provides many of Ann Arbor's top attractions, such

11

as the **Kelsey Museum of Archaeology,** a renowned collection of art and artifacts from Egyptian, Greek, Roman, and classical Mediterranean cultures. On Saturdays in the fall, Ann Arbor is U of M football; the largest stadium crowds in the country (104,000) gather to cheer on the Wolverines.

But there is another side to this college town, one that children will appreciate, and it begins at the ❖**Ann Arbor Hands-On Museum.** This is no stuffy hall with an endless row of glass-enclosed displays. The entire museum is devoted to participatory exhibits—more than eighty on four floors— and the concept that kids learn by doing. Housed in the classic Central Fire House, the museum was dedicated on September 28, 1982, the one hundredth anniversary of the building. Inside, visitors try exhibits such as the sand pendular, a suspended funnel that you fill with sand and swing to make various patterns. There is also the bubble capsule, where participants step into a ring of soap film and slowly raise a cylinder bubble around them until it pops. Some exhibits use computers and deal with complex theories; others are as simple as the mystery boxes: A child sticks in a hand and attempts to guess what is touched. All the exhibits come with a printed explanation that is appreciated mostly by the parents.

The Ann Arbor Hands-On Museum (313–995–KIDS) is recommended for children eight years old and older. It is on the corner of Huron and Fifth Avenue, which can be reached by following Business US–23 (Main Street) from M–14 north of the city or from I–94 by exiting to US–23 and then to Washtenaw Avenue. Hours are Tuesday through Friday from 10:00 A.M. to 5:30 P.M., Saturday from 10:00 A.M. to 5:00 P.M., and Sunday from 1:00 to 5:00 P.M. There is an admission fee.

OAKLAND COUNTY

It's 4:00 P.M. in Birmingham and you're sipping tea from fine china in a setting that includes fresh-cut flowers, silver platters of cakes and other tempting edibles, a fire in a fireplace of imported Italian marble, and a tuxedo-clad piano player, er, excuse me, pianist.

Must be tea at the Townsend. The afternoon ritual, in all its elegance, takes place throughout the week in the ❖**Townsend Hotel**, the most affluent hotel in this ritzy suburb of Detroit.

Built in 1988, the hotel has eighty-seven rooms and fifty-two suites on three floors, and among its guests have been entertainers such as Madonna, Michael Jackson, Paul McCartney, and New Kids on the Block. Just about anybody who plays in Detroit stays at the Townsend.

Have afternoon tea here, and who knows? Maybe you'll see Billy Idol stroll in. It has happened before. From Woodward Avenue in downtown Birmingham, turn west onto Townsend Street, and the hotel is reached in 3 blocks. There is one seating for afternoon tea at 3:00 P.M. Call the Townsend Hotel at (810) 642–7900 for reservations.

The urban sprawl of Southeast Michigan runs its course to Pontiac, but from there the terrain changes quickly to the rolling hills, lakes, and woods of northern Oakland. A drive of less than an hour from the heart of Detroit can remove you from the city and bring you to the porch steps of a rustic cabin on a small pond in a wooded area where whitetail deer often pass by. ◆ **Roston Cabin** in Holly Recreation Area makes a weekend spent in the woods as comfortable and warm as sitting around the fireplace at night. The cabin is snug and tight but still rustic and secluded enough to make it seem like an adventure in the woods—even though the car is parked right outside.

Built by the Roston family as a weekend cottage in the early 1940s, the cabin was obtained by the park, which began renting it out in 1984. It's a classic cabin built with walls of logs, polished planked floors, and red-checkered curtains on the windows. There is electricity, and the kitchen features an electric stove and refrigerator as well as a table, benches, and a wood stove. The sleeping room is larger, with a set of bunks and an easy chair facing a fieldstone fireplace. Overlooking the cozy room is a loft, the warmest part of the cabin at night, with four more mattresses. Outside you'll find a vault toilet, woodshed, a hand pump for water, and a barbecue grill.

It's necessary to reserve the cabin in advance by calling the park headquarters, and, surprisingly, the most popular time to rent it is during the winter when families arrive to cross-country ski on the unplowed park roads around the lakes. The overnight rate for the cabin is $35, and reservations can be made by contacting Holly Recreation Area (810–634–8811). The recreation area is reached by taking Grange Hall road (exit 101) east off I–75.

13

Many people exit I–75 at Grange Hall Road and head west, however, to explore the historical town of Holly. Established in the early 1800s, Holly was a sleepy little hamlet until 1855, when the Detroit-Milwaukee Railroad reached the town, bringing immediate growth and prosperity with the twenty-five trains that passed through daily. Martha Street, near the tracks, was the site of the Holly Hotel, many saloons, and frequent brawls. In 1880 there was an uproar between local rowdies and a traveling circus that left so many beaten and bruised, the street became known as ◆ **Battle Alley.** The most famous moment in Battle Alley's history was on August 28, 1908, when Carry A. Nation, the notorious "Kansas Saloon Smasher," arrived in Holly at the request of the local prohibition committee. The next day Nation, with umbrella in hand and her pro-temperance supporters a step behind her, invaded the saloons, smashing whiskey bottles, clubbing patrons, and preaching about the sins of "demon rum." Nation created the biggest flurry at the hotel, where she entered the "Dispensing Room" and attacked the painting of a nude over the bar.

Today the residents of Holly celebrate the occasion with a **Carry Nation Festival** the second weekend of September, highlighted by a reenactment of that special day in 1908 along with a parade, arts and crafts booths, and much food, entertainment, and yes, a few swigs of the very stuff Nation campaigned against. Battle Alley and its hundred-year-old Victorian buildings have been restored as a string of twelve specialty shops that include antique markets both along the alley and on nearby streets.

The ◆ **Holly Hotel,** which was built in 1891 and suffered through two devastating fires, the second in 1978, has since been complete restored, including the painting of the nude. It is now listed on the National Register of Historic Places but no longer provides lodging. Instead, the hotel is a fine restaurant, known for both its classic and its creative cuisine, all set in a Victorian tradition that reflects its birth during the railroad era. The main dining room, with its pedestal tables, soft glow of gas lamps, and red velvet wingback chairs, is the stage for such entrees as medallions of beef with morel mushroom sauce, fillet of beef Wellington, and sautéed Michigan rainbow trout. The hotel also provides gourmet picnic baskets that include not only appetizers, dinner, desserts, and wine but also linen, flatware, candles, and a map of good picnic spots in the area.

The Holly Hotel (810–634–5208) is open for lunch Monday through Saturday from 11:00 A.M. until 3:00 P.M. and for dinner Monday through Thursday from 5:00 to 10:00 P.M., Friday and Saturday from 5:00 to 11:00 P.M., and Sunday from noon to 8:00 P.M. Dinner prices range from $16 to $22, and reservations are recommended.

Michigan has more than it's share of unusual bed and breakfasts. You can book a room in a lighthouse, on a two-masted schooner, at a farm, in a home that doubles as a microbrewery. Now you can also make reservations to spend a night at the country's first B&B train.

Coe Rail has renovated a pair of classic Pullman sleeper cars to offer people the opportunity to wake up on the rails. Owners claim their ◆ **Star Clipper Train** is the "first railroad to offer bed-and-breakfast service on rail."

If you don't have a night to spare, then just drop by for dinner. Coe Rail has also re-created the romance of dining on rail prime rib, seafood, or such entrees as Duet au Poivre Pork in the train tradition of elegance with sparkling crystal, fine china, fresh starched linens, and ever-changing scenery through the windows. Each evening features a three-hour rail excursion, with guests indulging in a five-course dinner while the train passes the new Depot Park in Wixom, the wooded West Bloomfield Bird Sanctuary, and Woodpecker Lake.

Star Clipper Bed and Breakfast (810–851–7957) is reached from I–96 by departing at exit 159 and heading north on Wixom Road to Pontiac Trail. Continue north on Pontiac Trail into Walled Lake. Coe Rail Depot is on Pontiac Trail just past the Maple Road intersection. The Star Clipper departs Tuesday, Wednesday, Thursday, and Saturday at 7:00 P.M., Friday at 7:30 P.M., and Sunday at 5:00 P.M. year-round. A night on the train, including dinner, is $119.50. The dinner excursion only is $52.50

MACOMB COUNTY

In the fall one of the favorite activities in Southeast Michigan is a trip to a cider mill. Parents pack the kids in the car and head out to the edge of the county where a river turns an old wooden water wheel. The wheel is the source of power for the mill that crushes apples to extract the dark brown juice and refine it into cider, truly one of Michigan's culinary delights. After viewing the operation, visitors purchase jugs of cider, cinnamon doughnuts, and sticky caramel apples and then retreat to a place along the river. Here they enjoy a feast in the midst of brilliant fall colors, in the warmth of an Indian summer, and with the fragrance of crushed apples floating by.

Cider mills ring the metropolitan Detroit area, but one of the oldest and most colorful lies right on the border of Oakland and Macomb counties west of Rochester on Avon Road (Twenty-three Mile Road). ◆**Yates Cider Mill** was built in 1863 along the banks of the Clinton River and began its long history as a grist mill. It has been a water-powered operation ever since, but in 1876 it began making cider, and today the water wheel still powers the apple elevator, grinders, and press as well as generating electricity for the lights inside. The mill is capable of producing 300 gallons of cider per hour, all of which is needed in the fall to meet the demand of visitors who enjoy their treat around the huge red barn or across the street on the banks of the Clinton River in the Rochester-Utica Recreation Area. Yates Cider Mill (810–651–8300) is open daily from 9:00 A.M. until 7:00 P.M. from September through November, and from noon until 5:00 P.M. Saturday and Sunday from December until May.

After May, Yates Cider Mill is closed, but there is another enjoyable attraction in Macomb County, the ◆**Mount Clemens Train.** Families purchase tickets in an old caboose that now doubles as a depot and then board a 1924 train car. A whistle and an "all aboard" from the conductor signal the start of a forty-five-minute train ride, which includes banjo music over the PA system and on most trips, an hour-long stop at the **Military Air Museum** at Selfridge Air National Guard Base. Here visitors can view a variety of exhibits as well as vintage navy and air force planes.

The caboose is located on Gratiot Avenue just north of Joy Boulevard in Mount Clemens. The train (810–307–5035) departs Sundays from mid-May to late September at 1:00, 2:00, 3:00, and 4:00 P.M. The 4:00 P.M. trip does not include a visit to the Military Air Museum. There is a small admission fee for the ride.

St. Clair County

This county is often referred to as the Blue Water region of Michigan because it is bounded by Lake St. Clair to the south, Lake Huron to the north, and the St. Clair River to the east. M–29 circles the north side of Lake St. Clair and then follows the river to Port Huron, passing small towns and many bait shops, marinas, and shoreline taverns advertising walleye and perch fish fries. The most charming town on the water is St. Clair, 15 miles south of Port Huron and a major shipbuilding center in the early 1900s. The city recently renovated its downtown section, centering it on ❖ **Palmer Park,** which residents claim has one of the longest boardwalks in the world facing freshwater. The favorite activity on the 1,500-foot riverwalk is to watch the Great Lake freighters that glide by exceptionally close, giving land-bound viewers a good look at the massive boats and their crews. The second-favorite activity is walleye fishing. The St. Clair River is renowned for this fish, and anglers can be seen throughout the summer tossing a line from the riverwalk, trying to entice the walleye with minnows or nightcrawlers.

Above the walkway is a wide, grassy bank filled with sunbathers, kids playing, and, in mid-June, the arts and crafts booths of the **St. Clair Art Fair,** a popular festival along the river. Call the St. Clair Art Association (810–329–9576) for the exact dates and times. The riverwalk ends to the north at the **St. Clair Inn,** a historic hotel that features outdoor dining in a courtyard overlooking the river.

Port Huron, a city of 30,000, is the site of the Bluewater Bridge, the international crossing between Michigan and Sarnia, Ontario. It is also recognized throughout the state as the start of the Port Huron–Mackinac Sailboat Race in late July. On the eve of the event, known as ❖ **Boat Night,** the downtown area of Water, Lapeer, and Quay streets, which border the docks on Black River, becomes congested with block parties. Sailors, local people, and tourists mingle in a festival that spreads throughout the streets, the yacht clubs, and even onto the sailboats themselves.

On the quieter side is the historical aspect of Port Huron with its many stately homes, one of which has been renovated into ❖ **The Victorian Inn.** Located at 1229 Seventh Street in a neighborhood of nineteenth-century mansions, the home was built in 1896 by James Davidson, who owned a dry-goods company in town. Two families purchased the home in 1983 and established a fine restaurant on the main floor, a pub in the

17

basement, and a place of lodging upstairs. Listed on the State Register of Historic Places, the home is an excellent example of nineteenth-century craftsmanship with its hand-carved oak woodwork, leaded-glass windows, and plasterwork and trim on the ceilings. Patrons enjoy their meals in one of three small rooms that make up the dining area, one with a massive fireplace. The menu changes every month but generally features entrees of beef, fish, and chicken and includes full explanations of every dish served. The dinners are excellent, and the dessert tray beyond the willpower of most people.

The restaurant (810–984–1437) is open Tuesday through Saturday from 11:30 A.M. until 1:30 P.M. for lunch and from 6:00

The Victorian Inn

to 9:00 P.M. for dinner. Reservations are required. Evening entrees range from $16 to $25, while lodging upstairs is $55 to $65, depending on the room, for double occupancy.

A short walk from the Victorian Inn is the ◆ **Port Huron Museum of Arts and History** (810–982–0891) at 1115 Sixth Street. The museum combines an art gallery with collections of natural history and artifacts from Port Huron's past. Included are bones and displays of the prehistoric mammoths that roamed Michigan's Thumb 10,000 years ago and memorabilia of Thomas Edison's boyhood home, which was located in the city. A popular attraction is the reconstructed pilothouse of a Great Lake freighter. All the furnishings were taken from various ships, and visitors can work the wheel, signal the alarm horn, and ring the engine bell. All around the pilot house is a huge mural that gives the impression you are guiding the vessel into Lake Huron. The museum, housed in a 1904 Carnegie library, is open Wednesday through Saturday from 1:00 to 4:30 P.M. There is no admission fee.

THE THUMB

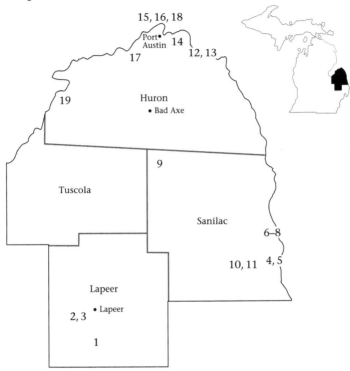

15, 16, 18

Port • Austin   14

17

12, 13

19

Huron

• Bad Axe

9

Tuscola

Sanilac

6–8

10, 11   4, 5

Lapeer

• Lapeer

2, 3

1

1. White Horse Inn
2. Lapeer County Courthouse
3. Past Tense Country Store
4. Charles H. Moore Public Library
5. Governor's Inn
6. Loop-Harrison House
7. Raymond House Inn
8. Bellaire Hotel
9. Petroglyphs State Historical Park

10. Croswell Berry Farm
11. Be Good to Your Mother-in-Law Bridge
12. Lighthouse County Park
13. Huron City
14. Grindstone Bar and Grill
15. Garfield Inn
16. The Bank 1884
17. Port Crescent State Park
18. *Miss Port Austin*
19. Bay Port Fish Company

THE THUMB

Within the mitten that is the Lower Peninsula of Michigan, there is a special area known as "the Thumb." The state's most recognized appendage is shaped by Saginaw Bay to the west and Lake Huron to the east. The bodies of water not only outline the peninsula but have wrapped it in rural isolation, the Thumb's trademark and the reason it is called "the getaway close to home."

Home is likely to be one of three of the state's largest urban areas: Detroit, Flint, or Saginaw, all less than a two-hour drive from the four counties that compose the region. Yet the Thumb is a world away. In this place where interstate highways give way to country roads and indistinguishable suburbs turn into distinct villages, the bustle and heartbeat of the city is replaced by the rural charm of the country.

You don't have nightclubs in the Thumb or dominating skylines or symphony orchestras. But you have more than 90 miles of lakeshore to view, small museums to discover, and an easy way of life whose rural pace will soothe the soul and rest a weary urban mind.

Lumber companies opened up the Thumb in the early 1800s, but after the trees were gone and the loggers had departed north, the region slipped into the small-town realm of agriculture. Today the area is still predominantly a farm belt, and from its rich soil come corn, sugar beets, grains, beans, and the lush grass that supports vast dairy herds and livestock. Huron County alone produces the most navy beans per acre in the world.

In recent years tourist dollars have become a significant part of the economy, but the region will never turn into one of the strips of motels and ice-cream stands that characterize much of the Lake Michigan shoreline, the heart of Michigan tourism. The Thumb lies on the other side of the state, away from the mainstream of summer traffic. And many travelers, who come for the fine beaches, country markets, and picturesque lighthouses, leave it cherishing that out-of-the-way character the most.

LAPEER COUNTY

A common misconception of the Thumb held by many Michigan natives is that the region is flat, without so much as a ripple between the shoreline of Saginaw Bay and the lapping waters of Lake Huron. A drive through Lapeer County dispels that notion immediately. The rolling hills that are the trademark of northern Oakland County continue north through the heart of the peninsula. In southern Lapeer County these hills have an enhancement that makes them unique in Michigan: the distinct white rail fences of horse country. Follow County Road 62 between M–24 and M–53 and dip south along the gravel crossroads of Blood, Garder, or Barber, and you'll pass through one of the greatest concentrations of horse farms in the state. Come in late spring when the grass is green, a new coat of whitewash covers the fences, and the mares and foals are trotting through the fields . . . and this area could easily be mistaken for the bluegrass region of Kentucky.

The heart of Michigan's horse country is Metamora, a small village of 500 that lies just east of M–24 and is crowned by the towering steeple of the Pilgrim Church (built in 1878). Settlers first began arriving in the area in 1838, but Metamora earned a spot on the map when it became a stop for a stagecoach route that later turned into the Detroit–Bay City Railroad in 1872. Whether travelers were carried by horse or by rail, the resting place was the same: a large rambling carriage house built in 1850 on one corner of County Road 62 and Metamora Road.

Back then it was known as the Hoard House, after its proprietor, Lorenzo Hoard, who charged travelers, weary from a long day on the carriage, only 50 cents a room. Today it's called the ◆ **White Horse Inn,** and while they no longer have rooms for rent, they are still serving meals 143 years later, making it the oldest operating restaurant in the county. One half of the inn is the dining room, completely sealed off from the barnlike barroom and decorated in dark oak, leaded-glass windows, and red plaid carpeting. On Thursdays both halves are filled with customers, as the inn offers its weekly all-you-can-consume fish fry for $4.00 per person. The rest of its menu is equally tempting, especially its White Horse Wellington, a flaky pastry filled with tenderloin, mushrooms, and cheese. The inn also has a list of daily seafood specials such as Rainbow Trout à la Praline, boneless trout dusted with a seasoned flour and sautéed in butter with pecans.

The White Horse Inn (810–678–2150) is open Monday through Thursday 11:00 A.M. to 10:00 P.M., Friday and Saturday 11:00 A.M.

to 11:00 P.M., and Sunday noon to 9:00 P.M. Menu prices range from $8.00 to $20.00 for dinners; reservations are recommended on the weekends.

North of Metamora along M–24 is Lapeer, a town of 6,270 and the county seat. Settlers began arriving in the area in 1828 and borrowed their village name from *la pierre,* the French translation of the Indian name for Flint River, which lies nearby. Lapeer became the county seat in 1831, and eight years later the county courthouse was built in the town common.

Lapeer is still the center of government, and the ◆ **Lapeer County Courthouse** still stands at the corner of Court and Nepessing streets. It is an impressive building featuring a Greek Revival style with four fluted Doric columns. It's topped by a three-tiered tower and a Roman dome and is noted as the "oldest courthouse still being used in Michigan today," even though the county has long since built a newer, all-brick building across the street. The old courthouse keeps its title because every summer the judge, the jury, and a handful of history buffs move to the other side of the street to hear a few cases in the second-floor courtroom of this landmark structure.

The first floor is now the Lapeer Historical Society Museum, and for a small admission fee, visitors can wander through the turn-of-the-century judge's chambers or the first sheriff's office in the county. The Courthouse Museum is open from early June until November 15. Hours are 1:00 to 5:00 P.M. Tuesday through Friday.

More history and a lot of country charm can be found just up the road from Lapeer at the ◆ **Past Tense Country Store.** The store is only minutes from downtown Lapeer and can be reached by driving north on M–24 and then turning east on County Road 7 (Daley Road). The first intersection on Daley is Farnsworth Road, and visible to the south from this intersection is one of the most impressive houses in the region. The huge, twenty-three-room home was built by the Farnsworth family, who were part of the first wave of settlers to farm the county. There are several buildings on the old farm, including the original barn that Lucie Hiner renovated into the Past Tense Country Store in 1971.

The store is an intriguing place, worth browsing through even if you are not in a buying mood. It is part country store, part antique shop, and part museum. Walk in on a chilly day and

Lapeer County Courthouse

the rush of warm air from the wood-burning stove greets you. Then you'll notice the one-hundred-year-old German barrel piano and the classic red Texaco gasoline pump next to it. The store itself is four separate rooms, each stocked to the rafters with such items as handmade baskets, dried flowers, candles, knickknacks, and children's toys, including one of the most amazing teddy bear collections you'll ever see outside a museum. Upstairs are numerous pieces of antique furniture, while one room is devoted to Christmas, with an old sled in the middle and walls covered with ornaments.

Above every shelf of merchandise, Hiner draws you back into the rural history of Lapeer with small artifacts she has saved. Above the wall of hard candy, a requirement in every country store, are rows of cleaning products and cans of food, all from an era long gone. Some you'll recognize, like Oxydol, Quaker Oats, or Calumet Baking Powder, though the packaging hardly resembles the modern-day counterparts. Many you will not (Quick Arrow Soup Chips or Red Moon Early Peas), for they have long since vanished from supermarkets.

Hiner and her family live in the Farnsworth house and operate the store, which is open Monday through Saturday from 10:00 A.M. until 6:00 P.M. and Sunday from noon to 6:00 P.M.

SANILAC COUNTY

M–25, the state road that leads out of Port Huron, follows the shoreline of Sanilac County and continues along the entire coast of the Thumb, ending in Bay City. While the road does not offer a watery view at every bend, there are more than enough panoramas of Lake Huron and shoreline parks to make it one of the more scenic drives in the Lower Peninsula.

Heading north on M–25, the first town you reach in Sanilac County is Lexington, which was incorporated in 1855 and boomed at the turn of the century. Back then the bustling town of 2,400 was a common stop for Great Lakes shipping and boasted an organ factory, a brewery, a flour mill, and six saloons. In 1913 the great storm that swept across Lake Huron destroyed the town's shipping docks and virtually isolated it. Lexington slipped into a standstill until the automobile and roads revived it in the 1940s, and today the town of almost 800 has worked harder than any other community in the Thumb to promote its future by preserving its past.

Lexington's streets are lined with turn-of-the-century homes and buildings, including four that are listed on the National Register of Historic Places. One of them is the ◆ **Charles H. Moore Public Library,** at the corner of Main and Huron streets next to village hall. The brick building was built in 1859 as the Devine Law Office but somehow passed into the hands of Moore, a local seaman who died in 1901, leaving the building to his three daughters. When a dispute erupted in 1903 as to where to put the town library, the daughters offered the former law office as a permanent site.

It has been the library ever since and today holds nearly 12,000 books, including a rare-book collection. Librarians will tell you that as many people wander through just to view the renovated interior as to check out a book. The wood trim and stained-glass windows have been fully restored inside, as has the graceful wooden banister that leads you past a picture of the "old seaman" to the upstairs. It's hard to imagine a more pleasant place to read than the sunlit room of the second floor, which features desks, tables, and office chairs that were originally used by the law firm.

The Moore Library (810–359–8267) is open Monday from 3:00 to 8:00 P.M., Wednesday and Friday from 10:00 A.M. to 5:00 P.M., and Saturday from 10:00 A.M. to 3:00 P.M.

Moore was also responsible for another building in Lexington that is known as a National Historic Site. When the seaman built his home sometime in the 1880s, he purposely chose to locate it just a block from the lake where he plied his trade. The huge Queen Anne–style home on the corner of Simons and Washington streets was constructed from white pine that loggers were shipping out of the port of Lexington. In 1901, Mary, the youngest daughter, used the house as a backdrop for her marriage to Albert E. Sleeper, a newly elected state senator. When Sleeper's political career led to his election as governor in 1917, the house became an important summer retreat for the couple, who were eager to escape the busy public life in Lansing.

Today the home is still used as a summer retreat. Bob and Jane McDonald purchased it in 1982 and the next year opened it up as the ◆ **Governor's Inn,** Lexington's first bed and breakfast. Although they gave it a new name and a fresh coat of paint, not much else has changed; it is easy to slip back to the early 1900s while staying at this inn. The three guest rooms upstairs are furnished with iron beds, Haywood-Wakefield wicker, and lace curtains that are draped across the nearly floor-to-ceiling windows. Guests spend summer evenings much the same way the governor and his wife did—on the wraparound porch in wicker rockers (there are seven now instead of two), enjoying the cool breezes off Lake Huron.

Reservations are recommended and can be made by writing Governor's Inn, P.O. Box 471, Lexington 48450, or by phoning (810) 359–5770.

From Lexington, M–25 continues north along the Lake Huron shoreline and in 11 miles reaches the next lakeside town. Port Sanilac began in the 1830s as a group of crude shanties for lumbermen and was known as Bark Shanty Point until residents decided in 1857 that the name of a famous Wyandotte Indian chief was a little more dignified for their community.

The town's most distinctive landmark is the Port Sanilac Lighthouse with its red brick house and whitewashed tower overlooking the town harbor and watery horizon of Lake Huron. Like Lexington, Port Sanilac's early history and wealth can be seen in the old homes that border its streets. One is the ◆ **Loop-Harrison House,** a huge Victorian mansion just south of town on M–25. The home was built in 1872 by Dr. Joseph Loop, who arrived in Sanilac in 1854 and began a practice that covered a 40-mile radius. The home and its extensive furnishings passed down through three generations of the family until Captain Stanley Harrison, grandson of the good doctor, donated it to the Sanilac Historical Society in 1964.

The Historical Society has kept the home intact, and visitors can wander through two floors of rooms that have remained virtually the same since the 1870s, right down to the original carpet, the cooking utensils in the kitchen, and the doctor's instruments in his office. There are also a dairy museum out back and a furnished 1882 pioneer log cabin. The Loop-Harrison House is open from mid-June through Labor Day from 11:00 A.M. to 4:30 P.M. There is a small admission fee.

Closer to town on M–25 is another impressive home that has become the ◆ **Raymond House Inn,** Port Sanilac's bed and breakfast. The home was built in 1871 by Uri Raymond, one of the founding fathers of the town, who established what is now Michigan's oldest continuously operating hardware store just up the street. The exterior of this Victorian-style home makes it hard to miss with its red brick facade, high peaked roofs, and white gingerbread trim. Inside, high ceilings, classic moldings, winding staircases, and large rooms add to the turn-of-the-century charm of the inn.

Shirley Denison bought the house after three generations of Raymonds had lived in it. Denison is a restorative artist from Washington, D.C., but she spent her childhood summers in Port Sanilac, where her grandfather was a local boat and lumber baron. She was enchanted by the antique furniture that filled the rooms, including the old-fashioned parlor and the six bedrooms she rents out on the second floor. In the rear of the house she has an art gallery filled with her sculpture and pottery as well as work from other local artists.

The inn is open from March through December, with a rate of $65 to $75 for double occupancy (private bath). Write to Denison at P.O. Box 43B, Port Sanilac 48469, or call (810) 622–8800 for a room reservation.

For dinner or what many say is the best fish fry in the Thumb, head almost directly across the street to yet another century-old Victorian home known as the ◆ **Bellaire Hotel.** Inside you'll find more arches, ceiling-high windows, and parquet floors. More important to the patrons, however, are the dining rooms and what emerges from the kitchen. Local people call them "porch dinners," for you sit in a glass-enclosed room overlooking the gardens that surround the hotel. Diane Douros, who has operated the Bellaire since she and her husband bought it in 1945, is best known for her perch and pickerel dinners. The meal is complete only if it is topped off with a piece of her tart lemon meringue pie. The Bellaire (810–622–9981) is at 120 South Ridge Road, and its entrees are priced from $9.00 to $12.00.

The stretch of M–25 from Port Sanilac to Forestville is especially scenic and passes three roadside parks on high bluffs from which you can scramble to the Lake Huron shoreline below. For those who want to explore the center of the Thumb, the Bay City–Forestville Road, the only intersection in tiny Forestville, provides a good excuse to turn off M–25.

Head west, through the hamlets of Charleston and Minden, and look for the "petroglyphs" sign at the corner of Bay City–Forestville and Germania roads. ◆ **Petroglyphs State Historical Park** is located just south on Germania and is marked by a large Department of Natural Resources sign. Situated in the wooded heart of the Thumb, the park features a large slab of stone with petroglyphs, Indian carvings that archaeologists believe to be between 300 and 1,000 years old and the only ones in the Lower Peninsula. The DNR has erected a large pavilion over the rock, which contains dozens of carvings. The most prominent one features a bowman with a single long line depicting his arm and arrow. There is no entrance fee. A short trail leads from the parking lot a few hundred yards inland to the pavilion.

Another reason to head inland in summer and fall is to pick berries—sweet, juicy, and back-breakingly close to the ground. Next to the town of Croswell is the ◆ **Croswell Berry Farm** (810–679–3273) at 33 Black River Road. This farm features strawberries from June to early July, then extends the picking season with blueberries, and finishes up the year with raspberries that are harvested as late as November. Hours are 8:00 A.M. to 6:00 P.M. daily.

One final reason to head inland to Croswell is to get some advice for keeping your marriage intact from a bridge that Dear Abby would appreciate. In the middle of this Sanilac County village is the ◆ **Be Good to Your Mother-in-Law Bridge**, which was first constructed in 1905 and has been rebuilt three times since then with David Weis, a local businessman, assisting in the effort.

Best known in town for offering sage advice to newlyweds, it was Weis who hung a sign at one end of the bridge that reads BE GOOD TO YOUR MOTHER-IN-LAW and at the other end one that says LOVE YE ONE ANOTHER. It's such good advice that the bridge has become something of a ritual with both newlyweds and long-time married couples, who are photographed under the black-and-white sign and then walk hand in hand across the structure.

They hold hands partly out of devotion to each other and partly to keep their balance. The 139-foot suspension footbridge is held up by four thick cables that make you bounce with each step across. The wooden slats sway, jiggle, and dip toward the Black River, coming within 8 feet of its murky surface. Some people are even more nervous about crossing the 4-foot-wide swinging bridge than strolling up to the altar.

Small tree-lined parks are at each end of the bridge, while a short walk away on Wells Street is the **Croswell Museum,** a former railroad depot that features a horse-drawn hearse, local artifacts, and plenty of fading photographs of the town's beloved swinging bridge. The parks and bridge are open daily from dawn to dusk. The Croswell Museum is open Saturday and Sunday from 1:00 to 5:00 P.M.

HURON COUNTY

The country charm of M–25 continues into Huron County as it winds north toward Port Austin on the "Tip of the Thumb."

Along the way it passes the small museum at ◆ **Lighthouse County Park.**

The museum is on the first floor of the classic lighthouse, which was built in 1857 and is still used by the U.S. Coast Guard to guide ships. The lighthouse actually overlooks two parks; the county park around it features seventy-four campsites with electricity for recreational vehicles, a swimming beach, a boat launch, and a picnic area. Out in Lake Huron is an underwater park, the Thumb Area Bottomland Preserve, which the state set up in 1985 to protect the nine known shipwrecks that lie offshore. Relics gathered from the wrecks will be stored in the Lighthouse Museum, which is open weekends during the summer. There is no admission for the park or the museum.

Where Lighthouse Road loops back to M–25 is the Thumb's most impressive attraction, ◆ **Huron City.** The town was founded in the mid-1850s by lumberman Langdon Hubbard, who needed a port for his 29,000-acre tract of timberlands, which included most of northern Huron County. It quickly became the largest town in the county, with several hundred residents and two sawmills that produced 80,000 feet of lumber a day. After the Great Fire of 1881 that swept across the Thumb devastated Hubbard's logging efforts, the lumber baron sold his land to immigrant farmers (after opening a bank to lend them the money), and for a while Huron City hung on as a farming community.

After withering away to a ghost town by the early 1900s, the area experienced a revival—a religious awakening, you might say—when one of Hubbard's daughters married William Lyon Phelps, a Yale professor and an ordained minister. Each summer the couple returned to Huron City and stayed at Seven Gables, the rambling Hubbard home, and eventually Dr. Phelps began preaching in the nearby church on Sunday. Local people soon discovered the magic of his oratory: simple solutions and relief from the problems of everyday life. The church that originally held 250 was quickly enlarged to 1,000 in the 1920s as people throughout Michigan heard of the preacher and began finding their way to Huron City for Sunday afternoon service.

Dr. Phelps died in 1937, but Huron City survived when the granddaughter of the founder preserved the community as a museum town. There are twelve buildings on the site, nine of them furnished and open to the public. They include a country store, a church, a lifesaving station, a settler's cabin, the old inn, a barn with antique farm equipment, and the Phelps Museum, which was built in honor of the minister in the early 1950s. Huron City (517–428–4123) is open July 1 through Labor Day, and the admission fee into the town includes an hour-long guided tour that tells the stories behind the buildings.

At this point M–25 begins to curve around the top of the Thumb, quickly passing a spur road to Grindstone City, which is named after the huge grindstones, some 6 feet in diameter, left on the beach from the days when this tiny town and its abundance of natural sandstone produced most of the world's grinding wheels. For an oral history of the era and the best hamburger in the Thumb, see Joe Mazzoni at the ◈ **Grindstone Bar and Grill** (517–738–7665) on Point Aux Barques Road near the public boat ramp. The restaurant is open from May through October for lunch and dinner.

Where Lake Huron and Saginaw Bay meet is Port Austin, the town at the "Tip of the Thumb." M–25 winds through the center of Port Austin and near its two busiest spots in the summer, the city marina and, just east of the marina's breakwall, delightful **Bird Creek Park,** with its boardwalk and sandy beach where people gather nightly to watch the sunset over Saginaw Bay. Travelers will find some antique accommodations in this New England–style town that boomed with lumber barons in the mid-1800s.

One of them is the ◈ **Garfield Inn,** a huge red mansion on Lake Street that is named after a U.S. congressman who stayed in the home in the 1860s and once delivered a stirring speech from its balcony endorsing Civil War hero Ulysses Grant for president. That man was James Garfield, who later became the twentieth president of the United States. The inn, which became a restaurant, bar, and bed and breakfast in 1985, has been named a national historic site, and among its more striking features is the mahogany bar and the winding cherrywood staircase that leads to the ten bedrooms upstairs, of which seven are rented out.

The Garfield Inn (517–738–5254) is open from the middle of April until January. Rooms based on double occupancy run from $75 to $85. The restaurant is open at 5:00 P.M. for dinner daily during the summer, on Friday and Saturday only during the winter.

In keeping with the restored atmosphere of the Port Austin

inns, there is ❧ **The Bank 1884** restaurant for, unquestionably, the finest dining in town. Built in 1884 as the Winsorsnover Bank on the corner of Lake and State streets, the red-washed brick building ceased being a place of financial business in 1957. In 1982 Anthony and Marilynne Berry began renovating the building, and two years later they opened its doors as a restaurant. The interior features stained glass over the classic stand-up bar, a teller's cage on the first floor, and walls of oversized photographs depicting early Huron County. The changing menu usually has shrimp scampi, prime rib, and En Papolote—walleye that is prepared with a crabmeat dressing and baked in parchment paper. The Bank 1884 is open daily during the summer except Monday, from 5:00 to 10:30 P.M., and weekends during May and after Labor Day until November 1. Prices for entrees range from $10.00 to $18.00, and reservations (517–738–5353) are strongly recommended for the weekends.

West of Port Austin, M–25 begins to follow the shoreline of Saginaw Bay and is especially scenic in its 19-mile stretch to Caseville. It passes many views of the bay and its islands, numerous roadside parks, and the finest beaches in the Thumb. One of the parks is ❧ **Port Crescent State Park,** popular with sunbathers and swimmers for the long stretches of sandy shoreline. The park also offers opportunities and facilities for camping, hiking, and fishing, and it contains the Thumb's only set of dunes, a unique place for beachcombers to explore. There is an entrance fee to Port Crescent State Park (517–738–8663) and a $14.00 charge to camp overnight.

Even more than for sand and sun, Saginaw Bay has always been known as an angler's destination for yellow perch. Visitors, especially families, without a boat or knowledge of where to go can still enjoy good fishing by joining a perch party boat. The large charter boats hold between twenty and forty anglers and usually depart twice a day for half-day fishing trips. In Port Austin, ❧ *Miss Port Austin* (517–738–5271) offers party-boat charters that depart at 7:30 A.M. and 2:30 P.M. daily. The fee is $25 per angler. You need to bring your pole; they provide the bait and take you where the perch are biting. Perch fishing is easy, and on a good day you may need a bucket to bring home your catch.

To enjoy your perch without having to put a minnow on your

hook, stay on M–25 as it curves southwest toward Bay Port. From the 1880s until the late 1940s, this sleepy village was known as the "largest freshwater fishing port in the world," as tons of perch, whitefish, walleye, and herring were shipped as far away as New York City and Chicago in refrigerated railroad cars. Today it honors its fishing past on the first Sunday in August with its annual Bay Port Fish Sandwich Day. The small festival includes arts, crafts, softball games, and lots of sandwiches—close to 8,000 are served during the event.

There is still a small commercial fishery operating in Bay Port, a place to go for fresh walleye, perch, whitefish, and herring. From the center of town, head for the waterfront docks of the ◆ **Bay Port Fish Company** (517–656–2131) for the catch of the day or to watch fishermen work on the boats or nets in the evening. The company, which is open from 9:00 A.M. until 5:00 P.M. daily, also sells smoked fish.

LAKE HURON

1. Curwood Castle
2. Union Station
3. Children's Museum
4. Labor Museum and Learning Center of Michigan
5. Penny Whistle Place
6. Chesaning Heritage House
7. Bonnymill Inn
8. Frankenmuth Brewery
9. Tiffany Biergarten
10. Bronner's Christmas Wonderland
11. Japanese Cultural Center and Tea House
12. Tridge
13. Bay City City Hall
14. Iva's
15. Lumbermen's Monument
16. Canoe Race Monument
17. Iargo Springs
18. Cedar Brook Trout Farm
19. Sturgeon Point Lifesaving Station
20. The Country Cupboard
21. Besser Natural Area
22. Fireside Inn
23. LakeView Hills Country Inn
24. Kirtland's Warbler Tour

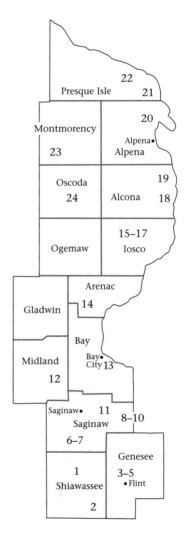

LAKE HURON

The Lake Huron shoreline, the eastern side of Michigan, is a region that has gone full circle in its history and its appearance. The first inhabitants of the area were Indians who traveled lightly through the woods and lived off the land but rarely disfigured it. When Europeans arrived, they were awed by what was perceived as an endless forest, woods so thick with towering white pines that the sun rarely reached the forest floor.

All that changed in the mid-1800s. Lumbering companies that had exhausted the forests in Maine were looking for pine to cut for new settlements on the Great Plains, which were desperate for wood in their treeless region. Michigan met those needs as the greatest lumber-producing state in the nation between 1850 and 1910, with an estimated 700 logging camps and more than 2,000 mills. Massive log drives filled the Saginaw and Au Sable rivers, which were avenues to the sawmill towns on Lake Huron. In mill towns like Saginaw and Bay City, sawmills lined the riverbanks, and huge mansions lined the streets as more wealth was made off Michigan's white pine than by miners in the Klondike gold rush.

By the turn of the century, all that was left were the stumps. The lumbering era had devastated the region, turning it into treeless areas that were wastelands of soil erosion. The Huron National Forest was established in 1909 along the Au Sable River, the first of many such preserves, in an effort to repair and manage the land. Lake Huron entered a new era in which terms such as *reforestation, conservation,* and *renewable resources* replaced the lumber lingo of *log drives, river rats,* and *clearcuts.*

Almost a century later the northeastern portion of the Lower Peninsula is once again a forested region. The trees are of a different generation and often a different species, but the effect on visitors is the same as when the first Europeans wandered through. To walk quietly among the towering pines in a forest padded by needles while listening to the gentle rustling of a coldwater trout stream is as much an attraction in this part of the state as sandy beaches or a cottage on the lake.

SHIAWASSEE COUNTY

In the early 1900s a young writer was tracking a grizzly bear he shot in British Columbia when suddenly the wounded animal appeared and trapped the man on a narrow mountain ledge. As the author would write later, "Sudden death seemed the hunter's inevitable fate. Then the huge bruin turned away, leaving the hunter unharmed. But not unchanged—the man packed away his guns and never hunted for sport again."

Instead James Oliver Curwood used the experience in his best-selling novel *The Grizzly King,* which was published in 1916. In 1989, when the book served as the basis of the movie *The Bear,* Owosso's favorite son—and one of its best-kept secrets—was finally exposed to the rest of the country. Curwood was born in the Shiawassee County town of Owosso in 1878 and returned with his family in 1891. After attending the University of Michigan for two years and working on a newspaper in Detroit, Curwood resigned to pursue literary work entirely in 1907.

He wrote thirty-three novels, most of them fast-paced tales set predominantly in northwest Canada, or "God's country," as the author called it. They were best-sellers worldwide and, between royalties and movie deals, they made Curwood a millionaire and allowed him to build ◆ **Curwood Castle** along the banks of the Shiawassee River in Owosso in 1922. Built solely as a writing studio, the castle features a great room on the first floor, where the author entertained guests; a twisting staircase leads to his work area upstairs. Today the castle is a museum devoted to the author, featuring memorabilia from Curwood's life, including his original writing desk, which is used as the reception center.

The castle, a replica of a French château, is part of the city's historical area, which also includes the first cabin built in Owosso. The museum (517–723–8844, ext. 554) is at 224 Curwood Castle Drive, which is reached from M–52 south of the Shiawassee River. The castle is open from 1:00 to 5:00 P.M. daily except Monday. There is a small admission fee.

At the turn of the century, Durand was what Detroit's Metro Airport or Chicago's O'Hare is today—the transportation hub of the Midwest. The first railroad, the Detroit-Milwaukee Line, arrived at the small town in 1865 because of Durand's central location, and, by 1907, there were seven different lines, promoting the construction of ◆ **Union Station,** a massive depot 239 feet long and costing $60,000 to build. It burned down two years later but was quickly rebuilt by Grand Trunk Railroad as the age of railroading and the town of Durand entered their golden eras. Almost half of the town's population of 2,500 worked for Grand Trunk, and more people changed trains in Durand than there were residents living there!

Union Station (517–288–3561), often called the "most photographed depot in the country," was recently designated the Michigan Railroad History Museum and Information Center. Visitors can wander through the station and view a gallery of railroading artifacts, including hand cars, engine lights, rolltop desks, and other furnishings of a 1900-era depot. Nearby is the town's **Railroad History Museum,** located in a 1919 Pullman baggage car. Every inch of the 80-foot car is filled with railroad artifacts, from a collection of conductors' brass buttons and keys, to an old depot bench and turn-of-the-century luggage.

Durand can be reached from I–69 by heading south at exit 116. The museum is off Saginaw Street at 205 Clinton Street. Union Station is on the south side of Main Street. The museum (517–288–3743) is open Saturday and Sunday from 1:00 to 5:00 P.M. May through October or by special appointment. A small admission fee is charged. The Union Station museum is open Monday through Saturday from 1:00 to 5:00 P.M.

GENESEE COUNTY

The heart of Genesee County is Flint, Michigan's fourth-largest city and the home of the Buick Division of General Motors. Fortunately, although its most noted attraction was Auto World, an ill-fated theme park that closed less than a year after it opened, the city has many other thriving attractions, including its delightful ◆ **Children's Museum.**

Described by its staff as a "touchable discovery center," the museum was proposed in 1980, and after six years of collecting donated materials, the center opened in 1986. Unlike other hands-on museums in Ann Arbor and Lansing, the exhibits are not complex demonstrations in science or physics. They're simply everyday items that children can touch, ride, climb, and make believe with.

The television studio is probably the most popular area. The news desk, weather map, and talk show set were actually used by Saginaw's WNEM-TV from 1981 to 1987 and then donated to the museum. The set is compete with real television cameras, control board, and monitors so children not only can give you the straight scoop on current events or weather but can watch themselves doing it as well.

If they'd rather play doctor, there's a hospital room with an elevated bed, patient gowns, doctors' coats, bandages, crutches, an instrument to check your blood pressure, and another to check your reflexes. Kids can also try their hand in the judge's chambers, appear on stage in costumes, or jump into a role as a bus driver, firefighter, or captain of a full-size boat, where even the life jackets are provided for a safe cruise on an imaginary Seven Seas.

The museum (810–767–5437) is located at 1602 West Third Avenue. Take I–75 to I–475 and depart at exit 8A to head west on Robert T. Longway, which turns into Fifth Avenue. Turn south on Grand Traverse Street and then west on Third Avenue. The center is open year-round from 10:00 A.M. to 5:00 P.M. Monday through Saturday and noon to 5:00 P.M. on Sunday. There is a small admission fee.

In the heart of Flint, there is a museum that shows an emotional seven-minute video of a strike that changed the course of history in Michigan, if not the entire country. This high drama of the Great Sit-Down Strike of 1937 is not surprising. Neither is the fact that Flint, a city bisected by the UAW Freeway, has the first and only museum in the state dedicated to the labor movement and unions.

The goal of the ❖ **Labor Museum and Learning Center of Michigan** is to tell "the story that the history books forgot," and in today's union-bashing times, it's obviously an uphill struggle. Developed to commemorate the Fiftieth anniversary of the Sit-Down Strike, this unique museum is neither flashy nor full of elaborate, hands-on exhibits, yet visitors who spend any time here depart with a better understanding of Michigan's history and, more important, why unions came to exist.

Inside you can see a "widow maker," the deadly one-man drill that miners struck over in the Great Copper Strike of 1913–1914, and also read accounts of workers coughing up wood dust in furniture factories or losing fingers in machine shops. One of the most dramatic pictures is of a woman breast-feeding an infant while working a sewing machine in a sweatshop of a garment factory. She was earning 8 cents an hour in the mid-nineteenth century.

The centerpiece of the museum is the exhibits devoted to the

Great Flint Sit-Down Strike, the forty-four-day ordeal that ended when General Motors agreed to sign its first contract with the United Auto Workers. Along with life-size photographs, the displays included voice-activated exhibits of police using billy clubs on strikers, the strikers' headquarters, and the office and desk of Governor Frank Murphy, who played such an important role in settling the dispute.

The Labor Museum and Learning Center of Michigan (810–762–0251) located in the Reuther Center's lower level, is reached from I–475 in Flint by departing at exit 8A and heading west on Longway Boulevard for a mile. Longway turns into Fifth Avenue, and at the corner of Saginaw Street, the museum is posted at the Reuther Center. Hours are 10:00 A.M. to 5:00 P.M. Tuesday through Friday and noon to 5:00 P.M. Saturday and Sunday. There is a small admission fee.

There's more fun for the kids just north of Flint at ❖ **Penny Whistle Place,** the unique contemporary play park administered by Genesee County Parks and Recreation Commission. Forget about teeter-totters, swings, and monkey bars. Park officials describe Penny Whistle Place as "a colorful, imaginative play area designed to encourage creative, unstructured play."

That's for sure. Modeled after highly successful parks such as Children's Village in Toronto, Michigan's first futuristic play area features Punch Bag Forest, where you run through an area of swinging, suspended punching bags, taking your best shots at them. There's also the Buick Bounce, a version of a moonwalk; the Cable Glide, which sends you flying across the park; and Together Toys, best described as giant Legos. Kids love the Net Climb, where they scramble across on all fours to reach a platform high above the park, and the Ball Crawl, in which they swim or sink through hundreds of thousands of colorful plastic balls.

This playground abounds with unique attractions. From I–75, follow I–475 and then depart at Saginaw Street (exit 13). Head north to Stanley Road, then east to Bray Road, where you head south to the entrance. Penny Whistle Place (800–648–PARK) is open Memorial Day weekend through Labor Day weekend daily from 10:00 A.M. to 6:00 P.M. Monday through Saturday and noon to 6:00 P.M. Sunday. There is an admission fee for adults and for children two years and older.

SAGINAW COUNTY

The only Michigan county without a natural lake, Saginaw County still has plenty of water, as the Saginaw, Tittabawassee, Bad, Cass, Shiawassee, and Flint rivers make it the largest river basin in the state, with 160 miles of waterway. It was these natural avenues and the vast forests bordering them that allowed the area to boom with loggers and sawmills in the mid-1800s. By the early 1900s the trees and loggers were gone, but reminders of the immense wealth they produced are seen throughout the county in magnificent Victorian-era homes, especially along the Boulevard in Chesaning, a major lumbering center on the Shiawassee River in the southwest corner of the county.

The Boulevard (part of M–57) and its historic homes were developed into the Old Home Shoppes, seven of the houses that are now gift and antique shops. At the beginning and the heart of it is the ❖ **Chesaning Heritage House,** one of the finest restaurants in Saginaw County. The house was built in 1908 by George Nanson as a monument to his family's lumbering business. Nanson's father, Robert, was born in England but arrived in 1852 in Chesaning, where he began as a farmer but ended up building a sawmill and, true to the American dream, became one of the wealthiest persons in the lumber town. The Georgian Revival–style house reflects all this with stately Ionic columns outside and the grand rotunda opening between the first and second floors.

The house changed hands a few times and was even vacant for ten years before Howard and Bonnie Ebenhoeh purchased it and opened up the restaurant in 1980. Dining is a leisurely affair in one of seven rooms on the first or second floor. Four of the rooms have fireplaces that are lit during the winter; another room is the original sun porch, now a glass-enclosed terrace that holds a half dozen tables. The Heritage House prides itself in the preparation of Michigan beef, and one of its specialties is baked tenderloin for two, which arrives with a crown of mushrooms. The dessert tray is also deliciously tempting and always includes an ice-cream sundae pie.

The Heritage House (517–845–7700) is open Monday through Thursday 11:00 A.M. to 9:00 P.M., Friday and Saturday 11:00 A.M. to 10:00 P.M., and Sunday noon to 9:00 P.M. Dinners range from $10

41

to $20. Behind the restaurant, the original carriage house has been turned into an antiques and gift shop with two floors of furniture, crafts, dolls, and a 1908 horse carriage on display upstairs.

Practically across the street from the Heritage House is ◆ **Bonnymill Inn.** The country inn is along the railroad tracks and overlooks a grain elevator.

But what did you expect?

The Bonnymill was originally the Chesaning Farmers Coop Elevator built in the 1920s to replace one that had just burned down. For more than half a century it stored the corn and soybeans of local farmers and loaded the grain into railroad cars until it was closed down in the fall of 1987.

Then it was renovated into a delightful inn that features twenty-nine guest rooms, of which eleven are suites featuring king-size beds, fireplaces, and in-room Jacuzzis; some even have wet bars. The center of the inn is a large atrium that includes a winding oak staircase, a spacious lounge, complete with a piano and fireplace, and an eating area where a hot breakfast buffet is served in the morning and tea in the afternoon. Outside is a long rambling porch that owners claim is "the biggest porch in mainland Michigan." (The longest porch in the state is at the Grand Hotel on Mackinac Island.)

Rooms at Bonnymill Inn (517–845–7780) range from $65 to $145 per couple. Special midweek packages include a voucher for dinner at the Heritage House.

Generally recognized as Michigan's number one attraction is the German town of Frankenmuth. "Little Bavaria" is famous for home-style chicken dinners served at one of two huge restaurants, **Zehnder's** and **Bavarian Inn,** which face each other on Main Street. What many visitors don't realize, however, is that Frankenmuth is home for the state's oldest brewery, ◆ **Frankenmuth Brewery,** which is located near the corner of Tuscola and Main streets. It began making beer in 1862 as Cass River Brewery and then became Geyer Brewing in 1874. The company was temporarily shut down in 1976, before reopening the following year under its present name with a German brewmaster arriving to direct the operation.

A state historic site, Frankenmuth Brewery (517–652–6183) offers tours of its plant year-round. Visitors meet in the Hospitality Center for a brief history of the company, a video of the beer-making operation, and a tour of the facility from brew kettles to bottling. They end up back at the Hospitality Center to sample the finished product. The tours are offered daily April through December from 11:00 A.M. to 3:00 P.M. on the hour. There is a $1.75 per person admission.

You can enjoy a stein of the local brew in almost every restaurant and bar in town, but the most intriguing place is the ◆ **Tiffany Biergarten** just north of Zehnder's Restaurant on South Main Street. The lumbermen's saloon is located on the first floor of the Hotel Goetz, which was built in 1895, when Frankenmuth was one of the leading logging communities in the Saginaw Valley. The tavern picks up its name from the eighteen Tiffany chandeliers, made in the 1930s. It is also adorned by a beautiful wooden bar, the original tin ceiling, the inlaid tile floor, and leaded stained glass. Tiffany Biergarten is

Frankenmuth Brewery

43

open from noon until 1:00 A.M. on Friday and Saturday, when there is live entertainment, and from noon until midnight the rest of the week.

Christmas in July? Only in Frankenmuth, where ◆ **Bronner's Christmas Wonderland** is home of the world's largest year-round display of holiday ornaments, decorations, trimmings, and gifts. More than 50,000 items are stocked in the huge 200,000-square-foot building that houses the store's showroom, warehouse, and offices. The business can be traced back to 1945, when Wally Bronner operated Bronner's Displays and Signs out of his parents' home and was approached by Bay City officials to decorate the city streets for the upcoming holiday.

Bronner created and built lamppost panels for the city, leading to more requests by other towns and eventually to his present business providing Christmas decorations to businesses, communities, and private homes. The store is an amazing trip into the spirit of the holiday, especially the religious aspect of it. Inside you will find more than 500 kinds of nativity scenes, figures from 1 inch tall to life-size; 260 Christmas trees decorated in such themes as sports or wildlife; and more than 6,000 ornaments from around the world. There are music boxes, every model of Hummel figurine ever produced, and, in the store's Nutcracker Suite, 200 different styles of wooden characters imported from Austria, Switzerland, and Germany.

You can't miss the store—outside it is surrounded by fifteen acres of painted snowflakes, twinkling lights, and the same kind of lamppost Bronner designed more than forty-five years ago for Bay City. Bronner's Christmas Wonderland (517–652–9931) is at the south end of town just off Main Street (M–83). It is open from June through December 24 from 9:00 A.M. to 9:00 P.M. Monday through Saturday, and noon to 7:00 P.M. Sunday. From December 26 through May, hours are 9:00 A.M. to 5:30 P.M. Monday through Thursday and Saturday, 9:00 A.M. to 9:00 P.M. Friday, and noon to 5:30 P.M. Sunday.

In Saginaw, near the Anderson Water Slide, an American creation, is the city's ◆ **Japanese Cultural Center and Tea House.** The house was actually built by Japanese artisans, who used no nails, only intricate traditional joinery and hand tools. Today the center is the only facility in the country where visitors can observe the classic formal tea ceremony.

The symbolic tea ritual is performed and interpreted on the second Sunday of each month beginning at 2:00 P.M. There is a small fee. The house (517–759–1648) and its tranquil gardens are located in Saginaw's Celebration Square, just north of M–46 at the corner of South Washington Boulevard and Ezra Rust Drive.

MIDLAND COUNTY

To most people the city of Midland is Dow Chemical Corporation, the place where Herbert Dow founded the company in 1897 that today gives us everything from Ziploc sandwich bags and Saran Wrap to much of the aspirin used in the country. But Midland is also a city of parks, with 2,700 acres in seventy-four parks scattered throughout the community for a total area that is three times larger than the average area most states allow for parks. The most famous of these is **Dow Gardens,** sixty-six acres of streams, waterfalls, small bridges, and beautifully manicured landscape next to Discovery Square, home of the **Midland Center for the Arts.**

Undoubtedly, the most intriguing is Chippewassee Park, site of the ◆ **Tridge,** the only three-way footbridge in the world, city officials proudly claim. The unusual bridge was built in 1981 over the confluence of the Tittabawassee and Chippewa rivers, and its wooden spans connect three different shorelines. In the middle they form a hub where benches overlook the merging currents of two rivers. The Tridge and the nearby riverfront area form the center of activity in downtown Midland. The Midland Music Society hosts free outdoor concerts in the park Thursdays at noon in June and July, which have unofficially become known as "Brown Bag-It Days," as office workers stream down to the area to enjoy their lunch break.

Also located near the Tridge is the Midland Farmer's Market and its 4-H Club petting zoo for children (open Sundays in July from 1:00 to 4:00 P.M.) as well as a city-operated canoe livery for a leisurely paddle up the river of your choice. The canoes are rented Saturday and Sunday from 10:00 A.M. to 7:00 P.M. in April and May and during the week from 2:00 to 7:00 P.M. June through September. The zoo is free, but there is a rental fee for the canoes. In the rest of Chippewassee Park, you'll find a fitness trail, a riverwalk, a picnic area, and an elaborate wooden playscape for children.

45

Bay County

The shoreline of Saginaw Bay was the final destination for much of the lumber from the valley, as thirty-two sawmills were clustered on the waterfront of Bay City. The city flourished on money from timber and shipbuilding, and a drive down Center Avenue shows where much of it went. The lumber barons seemed infatuated with building the most elaborate homes they could afford, and the restored mansions in this historic district overwhelm visitors. In the middle of this Victorian-era street is the **Historical Museum of Bay County** (517–893–5733), which spins the story of Bay City's golden era through three-dimensional exhibits.

More impressive than the grand homes, however, is the ❖ **Bay City City Hall.** Built in 1894, the Romanesque-style stone building dominates the city skyline with its 125-foot clock tower at the southeast corner. It was listed in the National Register of Historic Places, and in 1976 the building underwent major renovation that preserved the original woodwork and distinctive metal pillars in the huge lobby. Visitors are welcome to stroll throughout the massive structure and view the 31-foot Chmielewska Tapestry that hangs in the council chambers. Woven with hand-dyed yarns of 500 colors by a young artist from Poland, the tapestry depicts the historic buildings of the community. A climb of sixty-eight steps up the clock tower brings you to a most impressive view of Bay City, the Saginaw River, and the surrounding countryside.

The City Hall (517–894–8147) is located downtown at 301 Washington Avenue and is open from 8:00 A.M. to 5:00 P.M. Monday through Friday. Inquire at the Personnel Office in Room 308 for a trip up to the clock tower. There is no admission fee.

Arenac County

❖ **Iva's,** in Sterling, is not known nearly as well as the Bavarian restaurants in Frankenmuth, nor is it as large an establishment. Nevertheless, the old country roadhouse lacks nothing when it comes to serving a chicken dinner accompanied by bowls of homemade chicken noodle soup, hot biscuits, relish trays, and golden gravy that is ladled on scoops of mashed potatoes and moist dressing. The restaurant dates to 1938, when Iva Ousterhout began renting rooms in her large farmhouse to the oil-rig workers who were pouring into the tiny town to work in the nearby fields. Iva satisfied the hungry oil men at night with chicken dinners that always began with fresh birds from local poultry farmers.

That has never changed, but the house has. As travelers began hearing of Iva's dinners, the kitchen had to be rebuilt three times to accommodate the extra business, and additional dining areas were added. The house still resembles a roadhouse on the edge of a small farm village, and it still offers Iva's three original styles of chicken: southern (pan-fried and steamed), American

Bay City City Hall

47

fried (stewed, then fried in an iron skillet), and stewed. Steaks and seafood are also on the menu, but chicken is why travelers stop at Iva's.

From May through October, Iva's (517–654–3552) is open daily except Tuesday from 11:30 A.M. until 8:30 P.M. It is closed in November and December and open only Thursday through Sunday the rest of the winter. Sterling is 35 miles north of Bay City; to reach the restaurant depart from I–75 at Sterling Road (exit 195) and head east. Dinners range from $5.00 to $12.00.

IOSCO COUNTY

Perhaps the most famous river of the logging era was the Au Sable, which begins west of Grayling and ends at Lake Huron between the towns of Oscoda and Au Sable. In the 1890s it was assumed that forests were meant to be cut, and "driving the Au Sable" was a group of men known as "river rats" and "bank beavers," who floated logs down the Au Sable to sawmills on Lake Huron. A century later it's "downstaters," "flatlanders," and "fudgies" driving the river. Now, however, they're following the Lumbermen's Monument Auto Tour, an especially popular fall trip in Iosco County when tourists come to admire the color of the leaves rather than the size of the trunks.

Many begin the 68-mile loop at the Tawas Area Chamber of Commerce (800–55–TAWAS), where they pick up a free copy of the Lumbermen's Monument Auto Tour brochure. From Tawas City you head west on M–55 for a mile, then turn north (right) onto Wilber Road to reach Monument Road, which ends at River Road. A half mile to the east (right) is the entrance to ◆ **Lumbermen's Monument.**

The impressive bronze statue of three loggers was erected in 1931 and is now surrounded by trees very much like those they made a living cutting down. Even more impressive to many is the nearby interpretive area and museum, which gives a good account of the logging era with displays and hands-on exhibits. It puts into perspective the logger, viewed by many today as a colorful, Paul Bunyan–like character who ate apple pie and fry cakes for breakfast. In reality he provided cheap labor. In the middle of the winter, he made $2.00 for a twelve-hour day spent pulling a saw, while cold water sloshed in his boots. Little wonder that by the time most loggers turned thirty-five years old, they were too worn out or too sick to continue their trade.

The auto tour continues west along River Road and in 1.5 miles comes to ❖**Canoe Race Monument.** The stone monument, topped off by a pair of paddles, was originally built as a memorial to Jerry Curley, who died practicing for the annual Au Sable River Canoe Marathon. Today it stands in honor of all racers who attempt the annual 240-mile event from Grayling to Oscoda, often cited as the toughest canoe race in the country. From the monument site there is another fine overview of the Au Sable River Valley, and for those who keep one eye on the sky, bald eagles can often be seen in this area.

Still heading west on River Road, you reach ❖**Iargo Springs** in another mile. *Iargo* is the Chippewa Indian word for "many waters," and this was a favorite spot for members of the tribe who were traveling along the Saginaw-Mackinac Trail. It's almost 300 steps and eight rest stops down to the springs but well worth the exertion. The area below is pleasant and tranquil as the springs gurgle out of the moss-laden bluffs and into the Au Sable River under a canopy of towering pine trees.

ALCONA COUNTY

At Harrisville, US–23 swings away from Lake Huron and remains inland well into Alpena County. Taking its place along the water in northern Alcona County is Lakeshore Drive, the route to two interesting attractions. The first is ❖**Cedar Brook Trout Farm,** reached 2.5 miles north of Harrisville immediately after turning off US–23. Because of the almost perfect conditions for raising rainbow and brook trout, Cedar Brook was established in the early 1950s as the first licensed trout farm in Michigan. The key to the farm's success is the cold-water springs that flow from the nearby sandy bluffs. The water is funneled into the thirteen ponds and rearing tanks, and its year-round constant temperature (47 degrees) and high level of oxygen are ideal for trout. Its constant flow allows Jerry Kahn, the present owner, to manage without pumps. Kahn begins with eggs and raises the trout from frylings to rainbows that will measure well over 16 inches.

The bulk of Kahn's business is shipping thousands of trout in a tank truck to individuals and sportsmen's organizations for stocking their own lakes and rivers. He also lets travelers stop by and catch their own in two ponds, one stocked with rainbows, the other with brook trout. The water in the ponds is cold and clear, and below the surface you can easily see hundreds of fish swimming around. Throw some feed in the ponds (available from a coin-operated dispenser), and dozens of large fish rise to the surface in a feeding frenzy. Anglers are provided with cane poles, tackle, bait, and a warning that catching the trout is not as easy as it looks. No fishing license is needed.

Cedar Brook (517–724–5241), one of the few farms in the state that raises brook trout, is open for anglers daily from 9:00 A.M. until 6:00 P.M. from Memorial Day to Labor Day. The cost per trout depends on the size of fish caught, but for $3.00 or $4.00 and a little fishing luck, you can depart with a hefty rainbow.

From the trout farm, Lakeshore Drive continues north and in less than a half mile passes the marked side road to ◆ **Sturgeon Point Lifesaving Station** and the preserved lighthouse, built in 1869. The last lightkeeper left in 1941, but the U.S. Coast Guard continues to maintain the light. In 1982 the Alcona County Historical Society began renovating the attached lightkeeper's house and soon opened it to the public. The structure is a classic Michigan lighthouse, but the unique feature is that you can climb to the top of the tower (eighty-five steps) and not only be greeted by a panorama of Lake Huron but still view a working prism as well. Amazingly, all that is needed to throw a light miles out on the Great Lake is this huge work of cut glass and an electric light no larger than your smallest finger.

The lightkeeper's house is now a museum, with the five rooms downstairs furnished as a turn-of-the-century residence for those who maintained the attached tower. The four rooms upstairs are also open, and each showcases a different aspect of the county's history: shipwrecks, fishermen, the original lightkeepers, and perhaps the most interesting, the ice-collecting industry that boomed in the area during the winter so iceboxes could be kept cold in the summer.

The lighthouse is operated by a volunteer staff, who try to keep it open year-round Monday through Thursday from 10:00 A.M. until 4:00 P.M. and Saturday and Sunday from noon until 4:00 P.M. There is no admission, but donations are accepted to maintain the lighthouse.

Lighthouse at Sturgeon Point Lifesaving Station

ALPENA COUNTY

Lumbering turned Alpena from a handful of hardy settlers in 1850 into a booming town of 9,000 in 1884, and when the white pine ran out, the community sustained itself by becoming "Cement City," utilizing its huge supply of limestone. From the cement factories emerged Besser Manufacturing Company, the world leader in concrete block-making equipment. Today Alpena is a manufacturing center that can boast the largest population (12,000) and the only enclosed shopping mall in northeast Michigan. The residents of this modern community also value their past and have begun restoring the historic downtown area as Old Town Alpena.

The original shopping area is clustered around North Second Street and features small and specialized shops that could have been found here as early as the 1920s. One of the most unusual stores is ❖ **The Country Cupboard.** This antiques and general store is located in the old Sepull's Pharmacy, a landmark in Alpena from its opening in 1920 until Hutton Sepull retired in 1986. Outside, its aluminum facing looks plain, but inside it has the character of an old-time pharmacy, which catches unsuspecting visitors by surprise. There are the tin ceiling and the wraparound balcony on the second floor and the traveling ladders that lead up to the ceiling-high shelves stocked with old medicine containers, apothecary bottles, and boxes of tonic. On the ground floor the walls are lined with hundreds of wooden drawers, each holding some herb, tin of pills, or other merchandise left from pharmacy days.

When the store went on the market, Rita and Al Hess couldn't think of a better place to relocate their antiques business down the street. They filled the shop with collectibles, baskets, stained glass, and country gifts but kept the old pharmacy atmosphere intact and even began to restore much of the original woodwork. They still sell several of Sepull's more unusual or popular products, including Iceland moss (an herb for folk medicine) and the custom-blended Wellington tobacco.

The Country Cupboard (517–356–6020) is located at 102 North Second Street and is open year-round Monday through Friday 10:00 A.M. to 5:30 P.M., Saturday until 5:00 P.M., and Sunday noon to 4:00 P.M.

PRESQUE ISLE COUNTY

Jesse Besser, founder of the massive concrete block corporation, was also a humanitarian, and in Alpena the **Besser Museum and Planetarium**, the only accredited science, history, and art museum in northeast Michigan, is named after him. But Besser was responsible for leaving something in Presque Isle County—a small tract of land on Lake Huron whose towering white pines somehow escaped swinging axes of lumbermen.

The industrial genius, realizing the rarity of the uncut pines and the beauty of undeveloped Lake Huron shoreline, gave the area to the people of Michigan in 1966. Today it is the ◆ **Besser Natural Area,** managed by the Department of Natural Resources. The remote preserve, reached by departing US–23 onto County Road 405 to the south end of Grand Lake, offers a small niche of beauty and a little history in a quiet setting. Looping through the Besser Natural Area is a sandy 1-mile foot trail, which takes you past a small lagoon that at one time was part of Lake Huron. Look carefully at the bottom of the lagoon (you need polarizing sunglasses on sunny days) and you'll spot the hull of an old ship. The vessel served the community of Bell, which was located here in the 1880s and consisted of one hundred residents, several homes, a sawmill, a saloon, a store, and a school.

The most noticeable remains of Bell are the rock pier along Lake Huron, a towering stone chimney, and the collapsed walls of a building whose steel safe and icebox counter indicate it might have been the saloon. Toward the end of the walk, you pass through some of the oldest and largest white pines remaining in a state once covered with the trees. There is no fee to enter the preserve, nor is there a visitor's center or any other facility. Descriptive brochures that coincide with the footpath are available from a small box near the trailhead.

Visitors who depart from US–23 for the east side of Grand Lake, the state's nineteenth largest lake, with more than 5,000 acres of water, usually want to view lighthouses. They take in the beautifully renovated **Old Presque Isle Lighthouse and Museum** near the end of County Road 405 (Grand Lake Road) or **Lighthouse Park** at the very end of the road, where the tallest light tower on the Great Lakes is found, standing 109 feet tall.

The ◆ **Fireside Inn** is yet another reason to come to this part of the country, especially for anyone whose idea of a vacation in northern Michigan is renting a quaint log cabin on the edge of a lake. Fireside Inn began its long history as a resort when the original lodge was built in 1908, and the first few authentic log cabins soon began to appear around it. Little has changed about the lodge or the dining room inside with its rustic wooden beams, plank floor, and large windows looking over Grand Lake. They still ring a dinner bell to signal supper time and serve only one entree family style; afterward guests still wander out to the rambling porch, an immense sitting area 215 feet long, to claim a favorite wicker chair or rocker.

You can rent one of the cabins with a wood interior and stone fireplace or just a room (shared bath) in the lodge itself. Daily rates range from $30 to $40 per adult for the large cabins with three or four bedrooms. Or you can stop in just for dinner, a delightful experience in itself. Dinner prices range from $5.00 to $7.00, depending on what is being served that night, and you should call ahead if at all possible. The Fireside Inn (517– 595–6369) is located off County Road 405 at the end of the spur, Fireside Highway.

MONTMORENCY COUNTY

In the rugged hills that surround the village of Lewiston is ◆ **LakeView Hills Country Inn,** occupying one of the hilltops at an elevation of 1,442 feet. Following a steep drive to reach the resort, the inn looms above you. It is an impressive log and natural wood lodge with a fieldstone chimney and large windows on all four floors. Surrounded by trees and entrenched during the winter in deep snow, its most impressive feature remains the 165-foot-long porch. The verandah encircles the inn, passes every room, and features a variety of rocking chairs and swings where guests look down on the hills or gaze upon East Twin Lake and the village of Lewiston on its north shore.

Inside, the natural wood interior is accented by beams across the ceiling, polished oak floors, and a sweeping wooden banister leading to the rooms upstairs. Each of the fourteen bedrooms is furnished in antiques and has a different theme related to the history of Lewiston. The most popular room by far is on the fourth floor: the inn's observatory. The cubbyhole has large windows on every wall, a pair of rocking chairs, and binoculars to enjoy the view of more than 30 miles.

The inn is located just south of Lewiston, overlooking East Twin Lake. From Business I–75 in Grayling, head east on M–72 for 23 miles and then north on County Road 485 for 21 miles to Fleming Road, where the inn is situated to the west. Room rates range from $95 to $175 per night and include continental breakfast. For reservations write to LakeView Hills Country Inn at P.O. Box 365, Lewiston 49756; or call (517) 786–2000.

OSCODA COUNTY

The state bird of Michigan is the robin, but many argue that it should be the Kirtland's warbler. This small bird, the size of a sparrow, with a distinct yellow breast, is an endangered species that breeds only in the jack pines of Michigan. It spends its winters in obscurity in the Bahamas and then migrates to areas between Mio and Grayling, arriving mid-May and departing by early July. Only in these preserved nesting areas may birders and wildlife watchers have the opportunity to observe this rare bird, of which there are fewer than 200 breeding pairs remaining.

The nesting areas are closed to the public, but you can join a ◆ **Kirtland's Warbler Tour,** which is free and sponsored by the U.S. Forest Service office. The tour, which lasts from an hour and a half to two hours, includes a movie and discussion by a forest service naturalist and then a short trip to the nesting area. The guided group hikes through the jack pines, usually covering 1 to 2 miles, until they spot the warblers. Seeing a Kirtland's warbler is not guaranteed, but most tours do, especially in late May through June.

This tour is famous among birders, who come from all over the country for their only glimpse of the warbler, but it is also an interesting spot for anybody intrigued by Michigan's wildlife. The forest service office (517–826–3252), north of Mio on M–33, offers the tour Wednesday, Thursday, and Friday at 7:30 A.M. and Saturday and Sunday at 7:30 A.M. and again at 11:00 A.M.

THE HEARTLAND

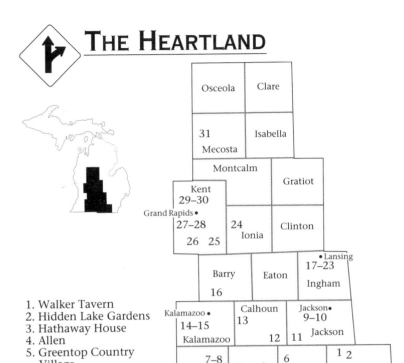

1. Walker Tavern
2. Hidden Lake Gardens
3. Hathaway House
4. Allen
5. Greentop Country Village
6. Litchfield Community Hand Tool Collection
7. Abbott's Magic Manufacturing Company
8. Colon Community Museum
9. Cascades
10. Michigan Space Center
11. Mann House
12. Homer Fire Museum
13. Binder Park Zoo
14. Kalamazoo Aviation History Museum
15. Celery Flats Interpretive Center
16. Gilmore–Classic Car Club of America Museums
17. Travelers Club International Restaurant and Tuba Museum
18. River Front Park
19. R. E. Olds Transportation Museum
20. Impression 5 Museum
21. Brenke River Sculpture and Fish Ladder
22. State Capitol Tour
23. Michigan Library and Historical Center
24. White's Covered Bridge
25. Fallasburg Covered Bridge
26. Ada Covered Bridge
27. Van Andel Museum Center
28. Fish Ladder Sculpture
29. Squires Street Square
30. The Corner Bar
31. Sawmill Canoe Livery

The Heartland

By the 1830s "Michigan Fever" had become an epidemic. Scores of pioneer families from the East Coast floated through the Erie Canal, made their way to Detroit, and then took to the newly completed Detroit-Chicago Road, which cut across the southern half of the Lower Peninsula. They soon discovered the rolling prairies of Michigan, where the soil was very rich and the land very cheap—the federal government was selling it for only $1.25 an acre.

From this onrush of settlers between 1825 and 1855, some of the state's largest cities emerged: Kalamazoo, Lansing, Battle Creek, Jackson, and Grand Rapids, all in this central region. But the Heartland of Michigan, the only area without direct links to the Great Lakes, is still an agricultural breadbasket. It is faded red barns and rolling fields of oats, the birthplace of Kellogg's Corn Flakes, and a village antiques dealer who scours area farms for the furniture and knickknacks that fill her store.

The vibrant cities, each with a distinct downtown that never sleeps, are popular destinations for travelers who can zip from one to the next on interstate highways six lanes wide. But the unique nature of this region is found by rambling along its two-lane county roads, which take you past the horse-drawn carriages of Amish country, down main streets of small villages, and along roadside stands loaded with the summer's harvest. In these out-of-the-way places, you can sample the fruits of Michigan's Heartland.

Lenawee County

At the northern edge of Lenawee County are the famed Irish Hills, an area of green rolling hills with intermittent lakes and ponds. US–12 cuts through the middle of this popular area and has become an avenue of manufactured tourist attractions: miniature golf courses and go-cart tracks, a dinosaur amusement park, another park called Stagecoach Stop U.S.A., motels, gift shops, and even an international speedway that holds Indy car races. So overwhelming are these modern-day sights that it's easy to pass by one of the most interesting attractions and probably the only one thaÙ is free, ❖**Walker Tavern.**

Walker Tavern

Located in Cambridge State Historic Park, the white clapboard tavern overlooks US–12, and rightfully so. The highway was originally an Indian trail and then became a stagecoach route known as the Detroit-Chicago Road. The stagecoach era lasted from 1835 to 1855, and on these rickety wagons, passengers traveled 50 miles a day with the hope of reaching Chicago in five days. The string of frontier taverns along the way was a crucial part of the system. They provided not only overnight accommodations (two or three travelers would share a bed for 25 cents a night) but also meals to the weary passengers who had just spent the day bouncing along the rough dirt road.

By the 1830s Walker Tavern had a reputation as a fine place to dine. Proprietor Sylvester Walker ran not only the inn but a small farm as well, while his wife, Lucy, performed miracles baking in the stone fireplace. A typical supper at Walker Tavern might include stewed chicken, biscuits, corn bread, and applesauce cake or pumpkin pie. The tavern still stands on its original site, and the pub, sitting room, and kitchen have been renovated. Next to the tavern is a reconstructed wheelwright shop, featuring the tools used to build and repair the fragile wooden wheels as well as the covered wagons and carriages of the era. Visitors begin the self-guided walking tour at the Interpretive Center with a film in its theater and an exhibit on the settling of Michigan.

Cambridge State Historical Park (517–467–4414) is on the corner of US–12 and M–50, 25 miles south of Jackson. The tavern complex is open from 11:30 A.M. to 4:00 P.M. daily from Memorial Day through Labor Day and by appointment through October 15.

Also located in the Irish Hills is Lenawee County's other outstanding attraction, ◆ **Hidden Lake Gardens.** Glaciers were responsible for the rolling terrain of the gardens, and when the ice sheet finally melted away, it left a topography of prominent knolls, ridges, valleys, and funnel-like depressions. Harry A. Fee was responsible for preserving it. The Adrian businessman fell in love with the scenic land formations and in 1926 purchased 226 acres, including its namesake lake.

He began developing the landscape and supervising its early plantings before giving the gardens to Michigan State University in 1945. The visitor's center was added in 1966, the plant conservatory four years later, and today Hidden Lake Gardens covers 670 acres with 6 miles of picturesque, winding, one-way roads, 5 miles of hiking trails to its remote corners, and more than 2,500 introduced species of plants.

Upon entering the gardens most people head for the visitor's center, which includes an orientation and information area, a gift shop, and a walk-through exhibit concourse. Next door is the plant conservatory, where 8,000 square feet of glass houses plants from around the world. Along with the kumquats and vanilla plants in the tropical house and the old-man cacti in the arid dome, there is the 80-by-36-foot temperate house used to display unusual houseplants and seasonal flowers.

From the conservatory visitors can follow a winding drive around Hidden Lake and then ascend through a unique forest carpeted in ivy before topping out at Gobblers Knob with a view of the surrounding ridges and hardwood trees below. The network of one-way roads also leads visitors past a glacial pothole, through an oak upland forest, around an open meadow, and ends, of course, at a picnic area.

The entrance to the gardens (517–431–2060) is located on M–50, 2 miles west of Tipton or 7 miles west of Tecumseh. The gardens, visitor's center, and plant conservatory are open daily from 8:00 A.M. to dusk April through October and 8:00 A.M. to 4:00 P.M. November through March. There is a small per-person admission fee.

There are many mansions-turned restaurants in Michigan, but few evoke an aura of gracious living and fine dining the way the ◆Hathaway House does. A National Historic Site, the home was built by David Carpenter, who arrived in Blissfield in 1836 as a twenty-one-year-old with $25. Seventeen years later, Carpenter was a wealthy merchant, and he decided to build a home that would reflect his position as one of the county's most prominent citizens.

The eighteen-room Hathaway House resembles a southern mansion. Inside guests are seated in six distinctively decorated rooms that were previouly the east and west parlors, the card room, and the library, among others. In this restaurant, you can still run your hand along the original cherry banister of the sweeping staircase, be warmed during the winter by one of five fireplaces, and admire the classic woodwork.

Afterward you can drop in at the Main Street Stable. What used to be the carriage house in the back of Carpenter's mansion is now a lively little pub that still features a rustic interior of hand-hewn beams, wooden benches, and lanterns hanging from the ceiling.

The Hathaway House (517–486–2141) is reached from US–23 by taking exit 5 and heading 10 miles west on US–223. Hours are 11:30 A.M. to 9:00 P.M. Tuesday through Thursday, until 10:00 P.M. Friday and Saturday, and noon to 8:00 P.M. Sunday. Dinner entrees range from $13 to $20.

HILLSDALE COUNTY

In 1827, a surveying crew from the Detroit-Chicago Road was working in the fertile prairie of the St. Joseph Valley when one crew member, Captain Moses Allen, fell in love with the area. His homestead led to a small hamlet of homes and shops known as Allen's Prairie, the first white settlement west of Tecumseh. This is the birthplace of Hillsdale County, but today ✦ **Allen** is better known as the "Antiques Capital of Michigan."

It began as a weekend flea market in the late 1960s and soon drew crowds of antiques hunters from several states to the junction of US–12 and M–49. Eventually some of the antiques dealers who rented the summer stalls began to set up permanent businesses in Allen. Today this quaint village of fewer than 300 residents supports more than a dozen antiques malls, each housing several dealers and other shops along a mile-long stretch of US–12, the town's main street. Some of the shops are located in red brick buildings near the intersection, others in old homes or weathered barns that are packed with furniture and other large antiques.

The largest shop is ✦ **Greentop Country Village** (517–869–2100), an antiques mall that consists of more than forty dealers displaying their wares in a dozen buildings. The best times to visit Allen are on the weekends of Memorial Day, Fourth of July, or Labor Day when the community holds open-air antiques festivals and even more dealers converge on the town and set up booths along the streets.

If you are heading south to Allen, swing through the picturesque village of Litchfield 14 miles to the north at the other end of M–49. Near the center of town is the Litchfield Town Hall, and featured in the huge storefront display windows is the ✦ **Litchfield Community Hand Tool Collection.** In one window there are seventy-five tools from the turn of the century, in the other another sixty-three, all numbered to correspond to a list taped on the window and in surprisingly good condition. In the three smaller windows on the second floor, more tools are hung in display as this town's collection continues to grow and grow. Someday they might have to use all these tools to build a museum for them.

The ✦ **Tristate Corner** in Hillsdale County is hardly a major tourist attraction. But there is enough interest in this geographical oddity that the Hillsdale County Historical Association maintains a stone monument dedicated to where three states come together, the only such spot in the Midwest that doesn't involve a river.

The monument is actually in Michigan, but it explains exactly where the corner is (130 feet to the south) because when you actually reach this obscure spot, a farm field on county dirt road, you want to make sure you're standing in all three states at the same time.

It's not as famous as Four Corners, the spot where Arizona, New Mexico, Colorado, and Utah come together, but, on the other hand, as the locals say, it won't burn two weeks of your vacation to visit.

From Camden, in the southwest corner of Hillsdale County, head south on M–49 and then west on Territorial Road. In less than 3 miles turn south on Cope Road and look for the stone monument on the left-hand side of the road.

ST. JOSEPH COUNTY

Michigan is known for many things, but to the average tourist, magicians and magic are not generally among them. Yet Harry Houdini died in Michigan, and the state has deep roots in the art of illusion and the related conjuring culture. One of the most famous American magicians in the 1920s, Harry Blackstone, toured the country with his act. At one time he passed through the village of Colon and then returned in 1926 and purchased property. Blackstone toured in the winter but spent his summers in Colon creating new illusions and rehearsing his show. One summer Australian magician Percy Abbott came to Colon to visit Blackstone and fell in love with a local girl and the quiet area. Abbott, eager to end his days of traveling, moved to Michigan and formed a partnership with Blackstone to begin a magic-manufacturing company.

The partnership went sour after only eight months, but the Australian magician went ahead with his plans and in 1933 set up ◆ **Abbott's Magic Manufacturing Company.** Today this sleepy farming village is home for the world's largest magic company, an interesting stop even if you've never done a card trick. The walls inside are plastered with posters and photographs of magicians, for all the famous performers, from Doug Henning to David Copperfield, have done business with this company. There is a display room within the factory, an all-black brick building, with cases and shelves filled with a portion of the 2,000 tricks and gadgets Abbott's Magic builds. And there is always a resident magician on hand to show you how they work.

A year after beginning his company, Abbott also instituted an open house for magicians as a sales incentive, and that quickly evolved into Colon's annual festival, Magical Get-Together. Every August more than a thousand amateur and professional magicians flood the village for a series of shows at the high school auditorium. Abbott's Magic Manufacturing Company (616–432–3235) is at 124 St. Joseph Street, 1 block off M–86, and is open from 8:00 A.M. until 5:00 P.M. Monday through Friday and until 4:00 P.M. on Saturday.

More magical memorabilia can be viewed at the ◆**Colon Community Museum,** which is housed in an 1893 church at 219 North Blackstone Road. Although many artifacts deal with the town's first pioneer families, one area is devoted to the personal items and photographs of Blackstone and Abbott. The museum is open Tuesday, Thursday, and Sunday from 2:00 to 4:30 P.M. There is no admission charge.

JACKSON COUNTY

The Lower Peninsula lacks the waterfalls that grace the countryside in the Upper Peninsula, but in Jackson they have their ◆**Cascades.** Billed as the largest manmade waterfalls in North America, the Cascades were a creation of "Captain" William Sparks, a well-known Jackson industrialist and philanthropist. They date back to the early 1930s, when Captain Sparks was developing a 450-acre park as a gift to the city and wanted it to showcase something different, something no other Michigan city had.

What he developed were the Cascades, a series of eighteen separate waterfalls with water dancing down the side of a hill from one to the next. Six fountains, varying in height and patterns, supply more than 3,000 gallons per minute, while 1,200 colored lights turn this attraction into a nightly event of constantly changing light, color, and music. The total length of the falls is 500 feet, and energetic viewers climb the 129 steps that run along each side of the Cascades, dodging the spray along the way. Others prefer to sit in the amphitheater seats to watch the water and light show that takes place nightly from Memorial Day to Labor Day.

The Cascades (517–788–4320) can be reached from I–94 by taking exit 138 and heading south for 3 miles. Signs point the way to the falls. There is an admission fee.

Jackson is home for two U.S. astronauts, Brigadier General James S. McDevitt and Lieutenant Colonel Alfred M. Worden. The two men and all astronauts are honored by the city at the ◆**Michigan Space Center,** located on the Jackson Community College campus. The center is a gold geodesic dome with an 85-foot Mercury Redstone Rocket at its doorstep. More than a dozen other rockets and engines grace the grounds around it, and inside the center visitors can trace the history of space flight from the earliest rockets to the *Challenger* disaster. Exhibits include the *Apollo 9* command module, the *Mercury* and *Gemini* spaceships, and even the capsule used to carry the first astronauts, chimpanzees.

There is an excellent display on astronaut suits, even the underwear they once used and the "bio-harness" they had to wear. Among the hands-on exhibits are a number of helmets visitors can try on, the glove box scientists used to handle lunar specimens, and a scale that will give a person's weight on Mars, Venus, Jupiter, the moon, or for those who care, Earth. Perhaps the most intriguing item in the museum is one of the smallest: Enclosed in a glass case is a slice from moon rock Number 15555. Around it are photos of astronauts picking it up and maps of its exact location on the moon, but it is the small grayish rock itself, the first piece of the moon most people ever examine, that commands most of the attention.

The Michigan Space Center (517–787–4425) can be reached from I–94 by taking exit 142 (US–127) south 6 miles to the M–50 exit. Turn left on McDevitt, and go 1 mile to the first traffic light; turn left on Hague and follow it 2 miles to Jackson Community College. The center is open from May to Labor Day. Hours are 10:00 A.M. to 5:00 P.M. Monday through Saturday and noon to 5:00 P.M. on Sunday. Call the museum for hours September through April. There is an admission fee.

Ten miles southwest of Jackson is the Victorian town of Concord, the proper setting for the ◆**Mann House,** a Michigan

Michigan Space Center

historical museum. The three-story house was built in 1883 by Daniel and Ellen Mann, two of the earliest settlers in the area. They raised two daughters, Jessie and Mary Ida, who continued to live in the house and maintained the original furnishings, most dating back to the 1870s. The younger daughter died in 1969 but bequeathed the historic house and all its contents to the people of Michigan through the Michigan Historical Commission.

The house can be toured today, and its eight rooms are a well-preserved trip back to life in the 1880s. The table is set in the dining room; a chess game waits to be played in the parlor; toys, books, and knickknacks fill the children's rooms. As soon as you walk through the wrought-iron gate at the street, you enter an era gone by. The Mann House (517–524–8943) is at 205 Hanover Street in Concord and is open from 12:30 to 4:30 P.M. Wednesday through Sunday from Memorial Day to Labor Day. There is no admission fee.

CALHOUN COUNTY

Homer is a small town in the southeast corner of the county, and its most impressive structure is a century-old gristmill on the banks of the Kalamazoo River. The U.S. government once wanted to turn the mill's black walnut beams into propellers for World War I airplanes. Another historic building in town, though considerably smaller, is a fun place to have breakfast on the Fourth of July: the ◆ **Homer Fire Museum.** The red brick structure with its arched windows and decorative cornice was built in 1876, five years after Homer was incorporated as a village. It has always been the classic fire hall on the main street, but in its early days it also served as a jail, town hall, and place for public meetings and local theater performances. It's the oldest building in town, and when Homer citizens decided to replace it, they preserved the old fire hall by attaching the new fire station to it.

In 1983 it was set up as a museum, with donated suits and equipment from former fire fighters. By far the most impressive item on display had always been there, a horse-pulled steam pumper built in 1887. Homer bought it from Union City in 1904 for $1,200 and placed it in the fire hall, where it has been ever since. The best time to see the displays is on the Fourth of July, when the town holds its annual Fire Hall Pancake Breakfast from 7:00 to 11:00 A.M. Almost 500 people enjoy the all-American morning meal in the new fire station on tables set up among the modern equipment. Then they wander into the old hall to see how fires were snuffed out in days past.

The museum does not have regular hours, but those who are passing through can go to the Homer City Offices (517–568–4311) next to the fire station, and an employee will open up the museum for you. There is no admission fee.

Battle Creek is best known as the home of Kellogg cereals and as the host of a hot-air balloon festival that draws hundreds of balloonists and thousands of spectators at the Kellogg Regional Airport. Although the famous tours through the cereal plants are no longer given and the balloon festival is not held every year, what you can count on visiting is ◆ **Binder Park Zoo,** one of Michigan's most unusual displays of fauna and flora.

The zoo is located south of the city in a wooded area along Harper Creek. Instead of a series of cages and animal houses in the middle of a city, Binder Park is a walk through the woods along boardwalks, brick walkways, and wood-chip trails, passing the animal exhibits that have been designed around the existing flora and terrain. There is the Northern Forest Boardwalk, where you can view timber wolves, great horned owls, and a Sitka deer; a Great Plains area, with bison, a prairie dog colony, and snowy owls; hungry trout that you can feed in Harper Creek; and a turtle log and viewing area in the pond.

In other areas you will see giant tortoises, zebras, cheetahs, and even a bald eagle, but the most impressive section is Binder's zoo within a zoo. The newest addition to the park is Miller Children's Zoo, the largest animal contact area in the state. Kids have a chance to feed and touch dozens of animals, including donkeys, rabbits, pygmy goats, draft horses, and pigs. Constructed around these contact stations are intriguing play areas. There's the Pig Pen, with models of pigs that children can play on; the dinosaur area, with a 100-foot-long brontosaurus and fossil-find pit; a giant spider web to climb; and a farm area with a silo slide and cow climber. Circling the entire children's area is the Z.O. & O. Railroad, offering rides on the scaled-down train.

Binder Park Zoo (616–979–1351) is reached from I–94 by taking exit 100 south along Beadle Lake Road and following the signs to the entrance. The zoo is open mid-April to mid-October from 9:00 A.M. to 5:00 P.M. Monday through Friday and until 6:00 P.M. on Saturday and 11:00 A.M. to 6:00 P.M. on Sunday. There is an admission fee.

KALAMAZOO COUNTY

The ◆ **Kalamazoo Aviation History Museum** is dedicated to the aircraft of World War II and the role they played in the Allies' success. It's a "living museum," for it not only displays many planes in its hangar on the southeast corner of the city's Municipal Airport, but it also restores them to working condition. Visitors are treated to exhibits and historic films in the video room and to a close-up view of more than a dozen historic planes inside and more planes outside. They can even watch mechanics work on restoring the latest acquisitions.

The museum has twenty-two planes, of which fifteen are licensed to fly, and the high point of the day is when one is wheeled outside and taken on a short flight around the airport. The times of the flights are posted each day, and people have an opportunity to watch the planes perform and to talk to the pilots afterward. Planes include a Curtiss P-40 "Flying Tiger" and three Grumman cats—"Wildcat," "Hellcat," and "Bearcat"—which led to the museum's nickname, the Air Zoo of Kalamazoo.

The Aviation History Museum (616–382–6555) is at 2101 East Milham Road and is open Monday through Saturday from 9:00 A.M. to 5:00 P.M. and noon to 5:00 P.M. on Sunday. You can drive to the hangar or, if you have your own plane, fly in. There is an admission fee.

Also on the edge of Kalamazoo is the ◆ **Celery Flats Interpretive Center.** The center is a truly unique facility that teaches the history of the efforts of Dutch immigrants to convert wetlands into one of the most productive celery growing areas in the world. From the 1890s through the 1930s, fields of green-tipped celery covered Portage, Comstock, and Kalamazoo; the celery was touted as "fresh as dew from Kalamazoo."

The historic area offers an 1856 one-room schoolhouse, a 1931 grain elevator, and historical displays on celery, as well as an opportunity to rent canoes to explore the surrounding wetlands.

Celery Flats (616–329–4518) is open May through September from noon to 5:00 P.M. on Friday and Sunday and 10:00 A.M. to 6:00 P.M. Saturday. From I–94 take exit 76A and head south 2.5 miles on South Westedge Avenue and then east a half mile on Garden Lane.

BARRY COUNTY

In 1962 Donald Gilmore, the son-in-law of Dr. W. E. Upjohn, the founder of one of the nation's leading pharmaceutical firms, was restoring a 1920 Pierce-Arrow touring car in the driveway of his Gull Lake summer home. The project dragged on into the fall, and by the time it was finished, Gilmore had to erect a tent around the car and light a kerosene heater. This was no way to work on a classic car. So Gilmore purchased three farms north of his home and then scouted the countryside for old wooden barns, which he had dismantled and moved.

The wooden structures held his growing collection, and in 1966 Gilmore opened his barn doors to the public on ninety acres of rolling farmland. The Classic Car Club of America added its collection to what had become the Hickory Corners Museum in 1984, and today the ◆ **Gilmore–Classic Car Club of America Museums** form a complex of twenty-two barns displaying 120 vintage automobiles in mint condition. The car that attracts the most attention is a 1929 Duesenberg. Some visitors, however, are fascinated with Rolls Royces, and the museums contain fifteen of them, including eight in one barn, ranging from a 1910 Silver Ghost to a 1938 Phantom III.

There is also a 1927 Bugatti Grand Sport Roadster, the "Gnome-Mobile" from the Disney movie *Darby O'Gill and the Little People*, as well as other transportation displays, including a full replica of the Wright Brothers' *Kitty Hawk* flyer. Those intrigued by hood ornaments can view a collection of more than 800 that captures everything from a windblown angel to an archer taking aim at the road ahead. They come from as far away as the former Soviet Union and include leaded-glass ornaments from France.

The complex (616–671–5089) is located on the corner of M–43 and Hickory Road, 7 miles north of Richland. From I–94, take exit 80 and head north to M–43. The museums are open daily from 10:00 A.M. to 5:00 P.M. mid-May to October. There is a small admission fee.

INGHAM COUNTY

What was once a hardware store and then an ice-cream parlour in the heart of old Okemos was turned into a restaurant in 1982 by Jennifer Brooke and William White, whose extensive travels around the world gave them a love for ethnic food. Food, however, was only White's second love. His first was playing the tuba, something he had been doing since he was eleven years old.

Adorning the walls of ◆ **The Travelers Club International Restaurant and Tuba Museum** are more than two dozen tubas—over-the-shoulder baritones and alto horns—and memorabilia that White has collected over the years, including a photo of the Great Band Race staged in London in 1918, basically five guys running and playing instruments at the same time. White's most valuable piece is the only known double E flat Helicon Tuba, which was made in 1915 and nicknamed "The Majestic Monster." His most unusual: the double Bell Euphonium; it has two horns.

The Travelers Club International Restaurant (517–349–1701) is reached from I–96 by departing at exit 110 and heading north for a few short miles on Okemos Road. Hours are 7:00 A.M. to 10:00 P.M. Monday through Thursday, until 11:00 P.M. on Friday and Saturday, and 9:00 A.M. to 10:00 P.M. on Sunday.

One of the best urban park developments in Michigan is Lansing's ◆ **River Front Park,** or as locals refer to it, RFP. The park is a greenbelt that stretches on both sides of the Grand River from Kalamazoo Avenue just north of I–496 to North Street, 3 miles downstream. A riverwalk, made of long sections of boardwalk near or on the river, runs along the entire east side of the park, with bridges that lead to more walkways on the west side. There are interesting attractions along the park, and you could easily spend an entire day walking from one to the next.

At the south end is the ◆ **R. E. Olds Transportation Museum** (517–372–0422), dedicated to the history of transportation in Lansing, where at one time or another fifteen different automobiles were manufactured. Almost twenty cars, from the first Oldsmobile, built in 1897, to an Indy 500 pace car, fill the old City Bus Garage along with old motoring apparel and other memorabilia. The museum is open Monday through Saturday from 10:00 A.M. to 5:00 P.M. and Sunday from noon to 5:00 P.M.

There is an admission fee.

Right next door you'll find ◆**Impression 5 Museum** (517–485–8116), which is described as an "exploratorium" for children and their parents, stressing hands-on exhibits. The 240 exhibits on several floors range from a music room filled with unusual instruments to be played, to a touch tunnel, where everything is explored using only your tactile sense. Impression 5 is open the same hours as R. E. Olds Museum, and there is an admission fee.

Continuing north along the east side, you'll walk under Michigan Avenue and past views of the state capitol, around Sun Bowl Amphitheater and the city's Farmer's Market (open Tuesday, Thursday, and Saturday), and eventually reach ◆**Brenke River Sculpture and Fish Ladder.** The structure is a swirl of steps and stone benches leading down to the fish ladder that curves its way around scenic North Lansing Dam. Come mid-September you can watch salmon and steelhead trout leap from one water ledge of the ladder to the next on their way to spawning grounds.

Riverwalk in Lansing

The park really comes alive during RiverFest, held Labor Day weekend, which includes, among other activities, a lighted boat parade and a fireworks display. On any clear evening there is a magnificent view of the capitol's lighted dome, shimmering over the Grand River.

For a closer look at Michigan's most famous government building, join a ◆ **State Capitol Tour** and be prepared for the building's stunning interior. In 1992, a major renovation of the century-old capitol was completed at a cost of more then $45 million. When the building was originally dedicated on January 1, 1879, it was one of the first state capitols to emulate the dome and wings of the U.S. capitol in Washington, D.C., and today it is considered by most as an outstanding example of Victorian craftsmanship.

All tours begin in the Rotunda, where visitors stand on the floor of glass tiles imported from England and stare at the stars in the top of the dome 172 feet above. In between are portraits of governors on the second level and, on the main floor, flags carried by Michigan regiments during battles from as long ago as the Civil War. Tours also include a look into the newly restored state Senate and House of Representative chambers as well as other offices and rooms, each accompanied by bits and pieces of Michigan's history.

To reach the state capitol from I–96, follow I–496 through Lansing and take the Walnut exit. State capitol signs point the way to the building and parking nearby. Capitol Tour Guide Service (517–373–2353) offers the tours every half hour Monday through Friday from 9:00 A.M. to 4:00 P.M. and Saturday from 10:00 A.M. to 4:00 P.M. Visits by groups of more than ten must be scheduled in advance. There is no charge for tours.

Almost as impressive as the state capitol is the ◆ **Michigan Library and Historical Center,** which opened in 1988. Nationally recognized for its architectural design, the 312,000-square-foot center houses the Michigan Historical Museum, The State Archives, and the Library of Michigan, the second largest state library in the country.

Most people, however, visit the center to see the museum. The Michigan Historical Museum features twelve permanent galleries displaying facades of a lumber baron's mansion and the state's first territorial capital, a walk-through tunnel of a copper mine, and an impressive woodland diorama. Other rooms feature a working sawmill, historic cars, a stake fort, and many other exhibits relating to the history of the Great Lakes State. To view the museum and the capitol is a full day for most families.

The Michigan Library and Historical Center (517–373–3559) is at 717 West Allegan Street, within easy walking distance of the capitol. Hours are 9:00 A.M. to 4:00 P.M. Monday through Friday, 10:00 A.M. to 4:00 P.M. Saturday, and 1:00 to 5:00 P.M. on Sunday. There is no admission charge.

IONIA COUNTY

When autumn arrives in Michigan and the leaves begin turning shades of red, yellow, and orange, many people instinctively head north to view the fall colors. But the southern portions of the state also enjoy their share of autumn brilliance, and one of the best drives is a 15-mile route that is lined by hardwood forests and rolling farm fields and crosses three covered bridges, including the oldest one in Michigan, ◆ **White's Covered Bridge.**

Nestled in a wooded area and spanning the Flat River, White's Covered Bridge was built in 1867 by J. N. Brazee for $1,700 and has faithfully served the public ever since. It is a classic covered bridge, its trusses hand hewed and secured with wooden pegs and hand-cut square nails. The bridge is 14 feet wide, 116 feet long, and you can still drive a car across it, though most travelers park on the other side and return on foot for a closer inspection. The bridge is reached by driving to the hamlet of Smyrna in Ionia County (5 miles southwest of Belding) and then heading south on White's Bridge Road.

Continue south on White's Bridge Road for 4 miles, and turn west (left) onto Potters Road for a short distance to Fallasburg Bridge Road, which will lead you over another covered bridge in Fallasburg County Park just inside Kent County. Brazee and his construction company also built the ◆ **Fallasburg Covered Bridge.** Its design is similar to White's bridge, and it was built with the same high standards that have allowed both these structures to exist for more than a century. Above both entrances to the Fallasburg Bridge is a stern warning: $5 FINE FOR RIDING OR DRIVING ON THIS BRIDGE FASTER THAN A WALK. The county park is a pleasant stretch of picnic tables and grills on the grassy slopes of the Flat River.

From the park, take Lincoln Lake Avenue south into the town of Lowell and head west on M–21 along the Grand River until you finally cross it into the town of Ada, where signs will point the way to the ◆ **Ada Covered Bridge.** The original bridge that crossed the Thornapple River was built in 1867 by Will Holmes but was destroyed by fire in 1980. The residents of Ada immediately opened their hearts (and their wallets), and the bridge was quickly rebuilt and restored. The Ada Bridge is open to pedestrian traffic only.

For those who like obscure historical sites, Ionia County has one of the best in the state. Located on the corner of Morrison Lake Road and Grand River Avenue, south of the town of Saranac, is the place known simply as **The Roadside Table.** It was at this very spot that in 1929 county engineer Allen Williams used a stack of leftover guardrail planks to build a table, the first public picnic table ever placed on a highway right-of-way. Today, of course, there are roadside tables and rest areas in all fifty states, and the only sights more common on our nation's highways are billboards and McDonald's restaurants. Along the road, the site is marked only by a small white HISTORICAL SITE sign, but a green STATE HISTORIC SITE plaque detailing the story has been erected next to the tables. The state still maintains the tables and garbage barrels, even though most of the traffic now flows along I–94 to the south.

KENT COUNTY

The favorite son of Grand Rapids is Gerald R. Ford, a local congressman who eventually became the thirty-eighth president of the United States. And although the **G. R. Ford Museum,** dedicated to his life and his days in office, has only been open since 1981, it is already the city's top attraction. More than a million visitors have passed through the center, which features two floors of exhibits and displays, including a full-scale reproduction of the Oval Office as it appeared in Ford's administration, gifts to the president from other heads of state, and an auditorium that shows the twenty-eight-minute film *Gerald R. Ford—The Presidency Restored.*

Long before the Presidential Seal was stamped on this portion of Kent County, Grand Rapids was known as the City of Furniture. In 1853 Grand Rapids was a small frontier town surrounded by forest with a seemingly endless supply of lumber and situated on the banks of the Grand River, which provided power for the mills. In this setting William "Deacon" Haldane opened a cabinet shop and soon was building not only cupboards but also cradles, coffins, and tables and chairs. By the end of the decade, there were several shops, and soon "Grand Rapids Made Furniture" became the standard of excellence in household goods.

As impressive as the Ford Museum is, it now has a rival practically next door. In 1955 the ◆ **Van Andel Museum Center** opened to the public, replacing the old Grand Rapids Public Museum. The $40 million structure is on the Grand River, and overlooking the water is its centerpiece, a glass pavilion housing a working 1928 carousel with hand-carved horses and a Wurlitzer organ. Rides are 50 cents, and it's debatable who has more fun—children or their parents.

Other exhibits in the three-story building include a replica of a Union Depot waiting room, a 76-foot finback whale suspended from the ceiling, an entire street from Grand Rapids a century ago, a high-tech planetarium, and many interactive and hands-on exhibits that focus on natural science and the unique western Michigan environment.

The Van Andel Museum Center (616–456–3977) is at 272 Pearl, just east of the Pearl exit off US–131. Hours are 9:00 A.M. to 5:00 P.M. daily. There is an admission fee of $5.00 for adults and $2.00 for children.

When the state began stocking salmon in the Great Lakes in the 1960s, the fish would spawn up the Grand River but had problems getting beyond the Sixth Street Dam in Grand Rapids. The solution was the ◆ **Fish Ladder Sculpture,** a unique sculptured viewing area that was designed by local artist Joseph Kinnebrew. Located at 606 Front Street Northwest, just on the north side of I–196, the ladder is a series of seven small ledges on the west bank of the river that allow the salmon to easily leap around the dam. The rest of the sculpture is a platform above the ladder that provides a close view of the large fish as they jump completely out of the water from one ledge to the next.

The first salmon begin arriving in early September, and the run is over in October. Local people say the third week of September is when you'll see the major portion of the spawning run. Spectators won't be the only ones there, however, as the river will be filled with anglers trying to interest the fish in a lure, a spectacle in itself.

Just 15 miles north of Grand Rapids is the small town of Rockford, which dates back to the 1840s, when a dam and sawmill were built along the banks of the Rogue River. Soon a railroad line passed through Rockford, and the town became a trading center with warehouses, a train depot, mills, and a bean-processing plant built along the river. What connected them on land was an unnamed alley that eventually became known as Squires Street. In 1970, the bean plant was renovated into the Old Mill, a cider mill and restaurant. This led to more historical buildings being bought and turned into a strip of specialized shops and stores.

Today ◆ **Squires Street Square** is the heart of Rockford, a charming 3-block section of more than forty shops and restaurants. You'll find stores in old warehouses, barns, a former shoe factory, a carriage house, even in railroad cars. Rockford Historical Museum occupies the Power House, which sits on the banks of the Rogue River and at one time was a generator plant for a local factory. All the businesses are within walking distance of each other, and most are open Monday through Saturday. Rockford can be reached from US–131 by taking exit 97 and following 10 Mile Road east a short way.

To travelers passing through Rockford, ◆**The Corner Bar** from the outside appears to be just that, a small-town tavern on the corner of Main Street and Northland. Once you step inside, you soon realize that this pub, decorated in brass nameplates, sports memorabilia, and newspaper clippings, is packed with history and hot-dog legends. For starters, the Corner Bar is the oldest brick building in Rockford. Built in 1873, the building survived several fires, including the "Great Main Street Fire" of 1896, and today is exceeded in age only by a wood-framed house behind the railroad depot.

At one time the building was a dry-goods store, then a hardware store, and finally, at the turn of the century, its most enduring business moved in. It became a saloon noted for its hot dogs. People came from all around to enjoy hot dogs served in steamed buns and topped with special sauce, a good heaping of relish, and chopped onions. Among the patrons one night in 1967 were several members of the Detroit Lions football team who amazed their waitress when they challenged each other to eat twelve hot dogs apiece. By the following year owner Donald R. Berg had turned that twelve-dog challenge into The Hot Dog Hall of Fame, Michigan's most unusual hall of fame, where twelve hot dogs at 85 cents apiece can immortalize your appetite with a brass nameplate on the wall. The present record of forty-two and a half hot dogs was set in 1982. The bar (616–866–9866) is open from 10:00 A.M. to midnight Monday through Wednesday, 10:00 A.M. to 2 A.M. Thursday through Saturday, and noon to 8:00 P.M. on Sunday.

MECOSTA COUNTY

Big Rapids may be the county seat for Mecosta County, but in recent years the city has also become known as the "Tubing Capital" of Michigan. Owners of ◆**Sawmill Canoe Livery**, which began renting out large truck tubes in 1979, say the portion of the Muskegon River that runs through Big Rapids from their livery to Highbanks Park is the most-tubed waterway in the state, with more than 30,000 people floating down every summer. It's easy to see why on a hot day. Tubing is a lazy and carefree way to beat the heat; you simply place the tube in the water, sit in it, and float. No special skills or paddle strokes are needed.

The run takes about two hours, and tubers often take small coolers (larger ones require their own tube) and plenty of suntan lotion with them. For $3.00 the livery provides the tube and transportation back from Highbanks Park, and on a hot August day there will be hundreds floating along the Muskegon at every bend. Sawmill Canoe Livery (616–796–6408) is at 230 Baldwin Street and rents tubes from May to September.

LAKE MICHIGAN

1. The Inn at Union Pier
2. Three Oaks Spokes Bicycle Museum
3. Warren Dunes State Park
4. Tabor Hill Winery
5. Fort St. Joseph Museum
6. 1839 Courthouse
7. *Idler*/Magnolia Grille
8. Wolf Lake State Fish Hatchery
9. Warner Vineyards
10. Saugatuck Chain Ferry
11. Mount Baldhead Park
12. Allegan County Historical Museum
13. Musical Fountain
14. Highland Park Hotel
15. Hackley House and Hume House
16. Gillette Nature Center
17. Grant Depot Restaurant
18. Loda Lake Wildflower Sanctuary
19. Shrine of the Pines
20. Silver Lake State Park
21. Sandy Korners
22. Bortell's Fisheries
23. White Pine Village
24. Nordhouse Dunes
25. The Lyman Building Museum
26. Ramsdell Theatre
27. Michigan Academy of Fly Fishing

Manistee

25–26   27

24

• Ludington
23   Mason

22

Lake

19

Oceana   18
20–21   Newaygo

Muskegon   17

• Muskegon
15–16

13–14

Ottawa

10–11

Allegan
12

7

Van Buren
8

Berrien   9

• St. Joseph
3   4   6

1   2   5   Cass

LAKE MICHIGAN

The Lake Michigan shoreline may be the Lower Peninsula's western edge, but many will argue that its heart lies in Chicago. The shoreline is now connected to the city by an interstate highway, but that only cemented what was already a long and enduring relationship between the Windy City and this watery edge of Michigan.

It began with the Great Chicago Fire of 1871, which left the city smoldering in ashes. Chicago was rebuilt with Michigan white pine, and the mill towns along the Great Lake, communities like Muskegon and Saugatuck, worked around the clock to supply the lumber. Maybe it was during these excursions to the sawmills that Chicagoans discovered that this region of Michigan possessed more than towering trees and two-by-fours.

They discovered the sand, the surf, and the incredibly beautiful sunsets of the Lake Michigan shoreline. By the 1880s, the tourist boom was on, and it was being fed by vacationers from cities outside Michigan, places like St. Louis, Missouri, and South Bend, Indiana, but most of all from Chicago. They arrived by Great Lake steamships, trains, and eventually automobiles. They caused luxurious resorts and lakeside cottages to mushroom, beginning in New Buffalo on the edge of the Indiana-Michigan border and continuing right up the coast: St. Joseph, South Haven, Saugatuck, Grand Haven, and Muskegon.

They call it the "Michigan Riviera," and even Richard Daley, Chicago's political boss and mayor, had a summer home on the strip. With the completion of I–94, the two regions were linked with a four-lane belt of concrete. Many Chicagoans, eager to escape the heat of their city, were less than two hours from the cool breezes of their favorite resort.

The Lake Michigan shoreline is still the heart of Michigan tourism. This incredibly beautiful region is characterized by great dunes and watery sunsets, but it's also known for its bustling resorts, streets full of quaint shops, and attractive beachfront hotels. The region lies on the western edge of Michigan, but Chicago's influence is unmistakably clear.

Just go to the beach and look at the license plates of the cars, listen to the baseball games the radios are tuned to, or see what city's newspaper someone is snoozing under. You're in Chicago's playland.

BERRIEN COUNTY

You barely cross the state border from Indiana before the first lakeshore communities appear on the horizon with their hotels and motels clustered near the water. Many are new, each with features little different from the one next door. But if you search a little, you can find an old inn from another era unique in its appearance and half hidden in a quiet neighborhood near the lake. If you search harder, you might even find ✦ **The Inn at Union Pier.**

Union Pier is a cluster of well-shaded streets and nineteenth-century summer homes about 10 miles north of the border. Locate Berrien Street and you'll pass the inn, three nautical buildings painted light blue with white railings. The inn began in 1918 as a single building called the Karonsky Resort, but business was so good that by 1929 two more structures were added. An easy journey from Chicago (today it is only ninety minutes by car), the inn thrived in the golden age of the Lake Michigan resorts but by the 1960s was abandoned and closed up. In 1983, Bill and Madeleine Reinke purchased the place, gutted it, and after two years of renovation, opened for business.

From the outside the most striking feature of the inn is the wraparound porch on one of the smaller lodges and the matching balcony above it, the place to unwind after a day on the beach. Walkway decks connect the buildings; one has a large hot tub, and tables for breakfast outdoors are on another. Most of the rooms are furnished in light pine and include a Swedish ceramic wood stove. The heart of the main lodge is a spacious common area with a grand piano, overstuffed chairs and sofas, and lots of literature. Guests begin each day with a full breakfast of local fruit and fresh baked goods on the deck and then head across the street to the beach, check out one of the inn's bicycles, or take to nearby roads for a winery tour or antiques excursion.

The Inn at Union Pier (616–469–4700) has fifteen rooms priced for double occupancy from $105 to $175 per night, which includes breakfast. Write ahead for reservations at P.O. Box 222, Union Pier 49129.

In downtown Three Oaks, in the southwest corner of Berrien County, is the ✦ **Three Oaks Spokes Bicycle Museum,** where displayed on the walls are a dozen bicycles, ranging from the Companion, a side-by-side two-seater, and a nineteenth-century model known as the Boneshaker (no rims, rubber tires, or inner tubes) to the Recumbent. This model doesn't look like a bicycle at all but was used in the spring of 1986 to set a world cycling speed record of 65 miles per hour.

The museum is much more than old bicycles and exhibits. What it really showcases is the southwest corner of the state, a pedaler's paradise called Michiana. Promoting recreational cycling in Michiana was the aim of the Three Oaks Spokes Bicycle Club when it was formed in 1974. The club developed the **Backroads Bikeway,** a selection of ten tours throughout the region that have been posted with color-coded bike route signs. The tours range from 8 miles in length to more than 50 miles and wind past sand dunes, wineries, cider mills, and one of the last stands of virgin hardwoods left in southern Michigan.

The museum was set up in 1986 and doubles as an information center. Along with the interesting historical displays, the center has an area for viewing videotapes on cycling and also has a reference library with stacks of information on tourist attractions in the area. You can even rent bicycles here. The Bicycle Museum (616–756–3361) is located at 1 Oak Street, in the old railroad depot 16 miles west of Niles on US–12 or 71 miles southwest of Kalamazoo. The center is open daily year-round from 9:00 A.M. until 5:00 P.M., and there is no admission charge.

The Lake Michigan dunes, the most spectacular natural feature of the region, begin in Indiana and hug the shoreline almost to the Straits of Mackinaw. The largest preserve of dunes in Berrien County is at ◆ **Warren Dunes State Park,** located on the lake 12 miles north of the state border. The park has more than 2 miles of fine sandy beaches and dunes that rise 240 feet above Lake Michigan. The dunes are a popular place in the summer for sunbathers and swimmers during the day and campers at night. What many don't realize is that Warren Dunes is the only state park that permits hang gliding and is considered by most gliders to be one of the best places in the Midwest, if not the country, for soaring.

Gliders are drawn to the park because of Tower Hill, which looms over the beach parking lot. They trudge up the hill carrying the glider and then soar into the winds from the top, flying over the sandy park or even above Lake Michigan. The sport enjoyed its heyday in the mid-1970s, when on a windy weekend there would be almost a hundred gliders on Tower Hill, with as many as twenty in the air at one time. The park rangers were so burdened with accidents from unqualified flyers that they instituted a certification system and stricter regulations for gliders.

What makes the park so attractive for these soaring adventurers, especially those just learning the sport, are the smooth winds that come off the lake and the soft and forgiving sand below. Gliding takes place year-round, but the best time is a weekend in the fall or spring with a wind out of the north-northwest. Arrive during those conditions and you'll see a half dozen or so colorful gliders in the air. Or, better yet, sign up for a one-day lesson from various glider instructors who set up school in the park. For an up-to-date list of the instructors, call Warren Dunes State Park (616–426–4013).

Lake Michigan does more than provide water for the beaches or a view from the top of sand dunes. It tempers the winter storms that roll in from the Great Plains and moderates the sweltering summer heat felt elsewhere in the Midwest. These effects, combined with the light soil of the region, have turned the lakeshore strip into a cornucopia of orchards, berry farms, and especially vineyards. Michigan is the third-leading wine-producing state in the country after California and New York. Paw Paw in Van Buren County is the unofficial center for the state's winemakers, with the largest vineyards, St. Julian Wine Company and Warner Vineyards, located right off I–94.

Smaller wineries are also found throughout the region, including a frequent winner in national competition, ◆ **Tabor Hill Winery,** in the center of Berrien County. The winery began when two Chicago salesmen who sold steel but loved wine brought a selection of hybrid grapevines back from France in 1968. They chose their vineyard site in the rolling hills of the county, hoping that the conditions were similar enough to those in France to ensure success.

They were. The transplanted vines thrived, and the winery produced its first bottle in 1970. Seven years later a bottle of its 1974 Baco won a gold medal in the American Wine Competition, and since then both the vineyard and Leonard Olson, the steel-salesmen-turned-winemaker, have won numerous awards. The

83

winery remains small, producing 40,000 gallons (or about 15,000 cases) of wine annually in almost two dozen types of whites, reds, and blends.

The best way to view Tabor Hill is on a walking tour that begins where workers bottle the wine and then heads out into the rows of trellised vines in the vineyard for a history of the grapes. You also descend into the wine cellar for a look at the huge vats and hand-carved oak casks that age the wine and then finish the tour in the tasting room for some tips on how to "judge" wine. The twenty-five-minute tour ends with everybody sampling Tabor Hill's finest wines.

The winery also includes an excellent restaurant with tables that overlook the rolling vineyard and a huge deck outside. A favorite activity of many, especially during fall, is to pack a picnic lunch and enjoy it on the open deck with a bottle of Tabor Hill. The winery also holds special events, including its annual Blessing of the Harvest around the first of September.

Tabor Hill (616–422–1161) is on Mount Tabor Road and can be reached from I–94 by taking exit 16 and heading north on Red Arrow Highway to Bridgman. From Bridgman head east along Shawnee Road and keep an eye out for the directional signs. This vineyard is definitely off by itself. The free tours are given noon to 4:30 P.M. daily.

In between the sand dunes, the orchards, and the wineries of Berrien County is a lot of history. Niles, the community of four flags, was the first settlement in the Lower Peninsula and claimed one of the first museums in the country when a private one opened its doors here in 1842. Eventually it became ◆ **Fort St. Joseph Museum**, and today it houses more than 10,000 historical items on two floors. Much of the museum's collection relates to its namesake fort, for which the French built the stockade in 1691. The British took it over in 1761, and the Spanish captured it twenty years later. In 1783, the Americans arrived and raised the fourth and final flag over Fort St. Joseph.

The museum's most noted displays, however, are devoted to the Sioux Indians of the Great Plains, not to the citizens of Fort St. Joseph. Many of the Indian artifacts were obtained by Captain Horace Baxter Quimby, whose daughter moved to Niles. While the U.S. Army captain was based in the Dakota Territory in 1881–1882, he became friendly with Sitting Bull, the most famous Sioux Indian chief. Among the gifts Quimby received from Sitting Bull were thirteen pictographs of the chief's greatest battles. The set of pictures is one of only three known collections of the Sioux chief.

The museum is right behind the Niles City Hall at 508 East Main Street. Niles can be reached from US–12, 23 miles east of I–94 or 33 miles west of US–131. Hours are 10:00 A.M. to 4:00 P.M. Tuesday to Saturday and 1:00 to 4:00 P.M. Sunday.

More history can be seen at Berrien Springs' ❖1839 **Courthouse.** The building that at various times was a militia drill hall, college, and even a church was repurchased by the county in 1967 and restored as the nineteenth-century courtroom where law was interpreted and justice dispensed in Michigan's early years of statehood. The classic Greek Revival–style structure is the centerpiece of the Berrien County Courthouse Square, a complex of five buildings that is listed on the National Register of Historic Places. It provides visitors a glimpse of the machinery of old-fashioned government.

Visitors can climb the wooden stairs to the second-floor courtroom where former Michigan Supreme Court Justice Epaphroditus Ransom presided over the first session in April 1839. Little in the building has changed since then. The wooden floors still creak as you approach the bench, and floor-to-ceiling windows still illuminate the courtroom furnishings of pewlike benches, wood-burning stoves, and the curved railing that separated the participants from the gallery.

The historic complex (616–471–1202) is located in Berrien Springs on the corner of US–31 and Union Street. Berrien Springs is 11 miles southeast of exit 27 off I–94. Hours for the buildings are 9:00 A.M. to 4:00 P.M. Tuesday through Friday and 1:00 to 5:00 P.M. Saturday and Sunday.

VAN BUREN COUNTY

South Haven has a long and colorful history spiced with Great Lake vessels and shipbuilding, and much of it is explained at the Lake Michigan Maritime Museum, which includes an outdoor boardwalk around several preserved boats. The good life on the lakes can also be enjoyed at dinner time aboard the ❖*Idler* at the **Magnolia Grille,** a restaurant floating in the Black River downtown in Old Harbor Village. The *Idler* was built in Clinton, Iowa, in 1897 for Lafayette Lamb, a lumber baron who used the 120-foot houseboat for his own personal enjoyment on the Mississippi. They never installed an engine in the *Idler*—Lamb didn't want to be disturbed by the vibrations—so the vessel was always pushed up and down the river by a small tug.

The *Idler* appeared in the 1904 World's Fair in St. Louis, but in 1910 it burned to the waterline. It was immediately rebuilt and eventually captured the fancy of actor Vincent Price's father. He owned it for fifty-eight years, and in a letter, now framed and hanging in the restaurant, Price said that what his father liked most about the riverboat was to play the piano on board. Eventually the boat was purchased, and it was brought to South Haven in 1979. Today it has been beautifully restored, and topside is the Bayou Beach Club, an open-air bar with sweeping views of the town and the Black River from every table. In the Magnolia Grille, located below, you can dine on white linen in either the original dining quarters or one of four staterooms. Each accommodates a party of six for a private gastronomic evening. The menu lists more than twenty entrees priced from $10 to $19, and every day six new entrees are featured. Many local people know the restaurant best for its Cajun dishes—blackened fish and steak, barbecued shrimp, and Louisiana steak salad—and its sinfully rich cheesecakes.

Magnolia Grille (616–637–8435) is open daily from 11:00 A.M. until 10:00 P.M. Monday through Thursday, until 11:00 P.M. Friday and Saturday, and on Sunday until 8:00 P.M. Reservations are accepted, and dress is casual on the riverboat.

Sport fishermen throughout Michigan head for the streams, inland lakes, and Great Lakes to fill their creels with a variety of fish. If they are passing through Van Buren County on M–43, they should also head for the ❖ **Wolf Lake State Fish Hatchery,** for this facility is one of the main reasons fishing is so good in Michigan. The hatchery dates back to 1928 and by 1935 was the largest in the world. Construction of the present facility began in 1980, and three years and $7.2 million later, the technological upgrading made Wolf Lake the finest complex for producing both warm-water and cold-water species in the country. No other hatchery in Michigan raises as many different species as Wolf Lake, which hatches steelhead, brown trout, chinook salmon, and grayling along with the warm-water species of tiger musky, northern pike, walleye, bass, and bluegill.

Hatchery tours should begin at its new interpretive center, which will fascinate anybody who dabbles in sport fishing. In the lobby there is a wall with plaques of Michigan's record fish—sort of a fishermen's hall of fame—plus displays of the trout fishing on the state's renowned Au Sable River. Off to one side is the "Michigan Room," a walk-through exhibit area that begins with an interesting series of habitat dioramas, cross sections of every type of water you might drop a line into, from trout streams to the Great Lakes. Each diorama shows the species that will be found, the habitat it likes, and the lure of a frustrated angler trying to land the lunkers that lie below. There are also exhibits on fish anatomy, slide presentations of Michigan's commercial fishery, and an area devoted to sport-fishing gear, including a delightful display of more than a hundred different historic lures, plugs, and other tackle. After viewing the exhibits and a short slide presentation in the auditorium, visitors are encouraged to wander through the hatchery itself to view millions of fish in the ponds and rearing ponds. If you want to see something bigger, ask for some fish feed at the interpretive center and walk out on the small pier at the visitors' pond. The small lake was developed so that people, especially children, could actually see some large fish. It contains, among other species, sturgeon, including one that is 5 feet long and weighs 55 pounds. Imagine that at the end of your line!

The center (616–668–2876) is open Tuesday through Saturday from 10:00 A.M. to 5:00 P.M. and also on Sunday from noon to 5:00 P.M. during the summer. There is no admission fee to visit Wolf Lake, which is reached from I–94 by heading north on US–131 for 4 miles and then west on M–43 for 6 miles.

Michigan is in no short supply of vineyards and wine-tasting rooms to visit, but few have the Old World character of ❖ **Warner Vineyards** in Paw Paw. The building itself is a Michigan Historical Site, constructed in 1898 as the town's first waterworks station. The vineyard purchased it in 1967 and proceeded to renovate the structure using lumber from old wine casks to transform it into a wine *haus* and bistro.

Today the brick and stone building is flanked on one side by a railroad dining car and reached by crossing a footbridge over the east branch of the Paw Paw River, which gurgles its way through

The Saugatuck Chain Ferry

the shaded grounds and around the outdoor cafe. The whole setting is one of idyllic enjoyment.

You can go on a wine tour or simply stop for a leisurely meal on the deck overlooking the river, on a brick patio alongside the dining car, inside the dining car if you wish, or in the quaint bistro itself.

Warner Champagne Cellar & Bistro (616–657–3165) is reached from I–94 by taking exit 60 and heading north on M–40 into Paw Paw. The winery is at 706 South Kalamazoo. From June through September lunch is served from 11:00 A.M. to 3:00 P.M. and dinner from 5:00 to 9:30 P.M. Dinner entrees range from $12 to $18.

ALLEGAN COUNTY

On the map Saugatuck looks like just the next beachfront community along the lake, but in reality it is a trendy resort whose streets are lined with fine restaurants, quaint shops, and lots of tourists. Perhaps the most striking sight in Saugatuck is the docks along the Kalamazoo River, where moored at the edge of the shopping district is an armada of cabin cruisers and sailboats 30, 40, or 50 feet in length or even longer. You can pick up the boardwalk that winds past the boats on the river anywhere along Water Street, and if you follow it north, eventually you'll come to the most unusual vessel afloat, the ♦ **Saugatuck Chain Ferry.** It's the only chain-powered ferry in the state, and it has been carrying passengers across the Kalamazoo River since 1838. An operator hand-cranks a 380-foot chain attached at each shore, pulling the small white ferry through the water.

It's only 50 cents for the five-minute ride, and it is your escape from the bustling downtown shopping district to one of the most beautiful beaches on the lake. Once on the other side, you walk north for a few hundred yards until you reach ♦ **Mount Baldhead Park,** with tables, shelter, and a dock on the river. There is also a stairway that takes you (after a little huffing and puffing) to the top of the 200-foot dune, where you are greeted with a glorious panorama of Saugatuck, Kalamazoo Lake to the southeast, and Lake Michigan to the west. On the other side you have a choice. You can descend to **Oval Beach** along the Northwoods Trail, an easy walk that includes a view of the lake and beach along the way. Or you can dash madly down the steep and sandy Beach Trail, right off the towering dune, across the beach, and into the lake for a cool dip.

Moving inland, another interesting attraction is the old Allegan County Jail in Allegan. Seriously. The imposing red brick building was built in 1906 and features Greek Revival architecture with a peaked roof and columns along the porch. There are bars on the windows, a hexagonal turret in the corner, and a three-story grandeur that is lacking in its newer counterpart across the street.

But most unusual is the small red sign on Walnut that says ♦ **Allegan County Historical Museum.** Go to jail and take a history lesson in penitentiary punishment. Within the museum are a variety of exhibits, including a country store loaded with

89

nineteenth-century merchandise, a display devoted to Allegan's General Benjamin Pritchard, whose men captured Confederate President Jefferson Davis during the Civil War, and a historical laundry room.

But coat hangers and wringers are not what draw more than 1,000 visitors to the museum every year. It's a macabre fascination with slammers and pokeys. To that end, a guide leads you through the sheriff's living quarters and the large kitchen, where his wife would prepare meals for up to thirty prisoners a night and then pass plates through a small door in the wall. On the second floor are rows of six-by-eight-foot cells, complete with the graffiti that disheartened convicts scratched on the walls in the 1930s. You can even walk through the maximum security cells, now filled with a historical toy collection, view the old padded cell, and examine the holding pen for "ladies."

The jail is open on Friday 2:00 to 5:00 P.M. from June through Labor Day or by appointment by calling Marguerite Miller at (616) 673–4853. To reach the museum, depart at M–222 (exit 55) off US–131 and head west into Allegan. The Old Jail is at 113 Walnut Street, between Hubbard and Trowbridge.

OTTAWA COUNTY

Grand Haven has developed its waterfront along the Grand River and includes a riverwalk that extends several miles from downtown to the picturesque Grand Haven Lighthouse out in Lake Michigan. But by far the most noted aspect of the river is the city's ◈ **Musical Fountain,** the world's largest, which performs nightly during the summer with electronically controlled and synchronized music. Performances begin around dusk (9:00 to 9:30 P.M.), and most people enjoy the free concerts by assembling in the Waterfront Stadium.

The Grand Hotel on Mackinac Island has always been famous for its world's longest porch, but at the turn of the century it had a rival in Grand Haven that boasted the "second longest porch in the world." The ◈ **Highland Park Hotel** was built in 1889 to become Grand Haven's premier hotel, serving tourists who were mostly from Chicago and St. Louis. It was situated on a bluff overlooking Lake Michigan, and its fifty-one rooms and long porch captured the gentle breezes and sunsets off the lake night after night. It had a superb dining room that hosted such legendary entertainers as Glenn Miller and his band. In 1967, however, the hotel caught fire and burned to the ground, leaving only the most northern section.

Houses now stand where there used to be a hotel, but the portion that was salvaged again offers travelers beachfront accommodations. Each of the six rooms has its own entrance and a private porch on the second floor, where breakfast is served. The hotel also hosts a social hour every evening on one of its two lakefront porches, because—despite the excellent breakfasts and historic atmosphere—its real specialty is sunsets, enjoyed most nights along with vintage wines and imported cheeses.

The Highland Park Hotel (616–842–6483, 846–1473) is open year-round and is right off Harbor Avenue, across from Grand Haven State Park. Room rates per night range from $60 to $120, and reservations can be secured by writing the hotel at 1414 Lake Avenue, Grand Haven 49417.

MUSKEGON COUNTY

In the late 1800s, this county was the heart of lumbering on Michigan's western side, and the city of Muskegon grew during the prosperous era to be known as the "Lumber Queen of the World." A drive down West Webster Avenue shows how much money was made and where much of it went: The Victorian mansions are fabulous. The most elaborate houses were built by the two men who prospered most of all from Michigan white pine, Charles H. Hackley and his partner, Thomas Hume. They built their homes next to each other, and it reportedly took 200 artisans and craftsmen two years to complete the houses. Behind the homes the men shared the same carriage house. The ◆**Hackley House** and **Hume House** are listed on the National Register of Historic Places and have been called two of the nation's most outstanding examples of Victorian architecture.

Although restoration continues, the homes are open for tours. The Hackley House is especially impressive, a virtual museum of carved woodwork that strikes you from the moment you walk into the home and are greeted by unusual figures along the walls.

91

Almost every aspect of the house is overwhelming, from its original furnishings and stained-glass windows to the hand-stenciled walls and the eleven fireplaces, each made unique with imported ceramic tiles. If you see only one restored home in Michigan, it should be the Hackley House, where it's hard to imagine living in such style.

The Hackley and Hume Historic Site (616–722–7578) is at 484 West Webster Avenue. Tours are offered May through September, Wednesday, Saturday, and Sunday from 1:00 to 4:00 P.M. There is a small admission fee.

The towering dunes along the eastern side of Lake Michigan represent the world's largest accumulation of dunes bordering a body of freshwater and are renowned throughout the country. One of the best places for learning how dunes develop and change is the ◆ **Gillette Nature Center** within P. J. Hoffmaster State Park. The center is in fact overshadowed by a huge dune best viewed from the lobby's glass wall to the west. The center features an exhibit hall entitled "From a Grain of Sand," which guides you through the natural history of the dunes, and an eighty-two-seat theater that uses a nine-projector, multi-image slide show to further explain their delicate nature. On the ground floor there is a gallery that offers hands-on exhibits to help children understand the environment of the park.

Most visitors view the exhibits and then hike up to the Dune Platform Overlook. The trail begins next to the center and includes a wooden walkway of 165 steps. It puts you 190 feet above the lake, with spectacular views of the surrounding dune country. There is a vehicle permit fee to enter the state park (616–798–3711), which is reached by heading south of Muskegon on US–31 and exiting at Pontaluna Road and heading west. The Gillette Nature Center is open during summer months Tuesday through Sunday from 9:00 A.M. to 5:00 P.M., during the rest of the year Tuesday through Friday 1:00 to 5:00 P.M. and weekends 10:00 A.M. to 5:00 P.M.

NEWAYGO COUNTY

The most distinctive structure in Grant, a southern Newaygo County town, is its wooden water tower. Built in 1891, it's the classic "Petticoat Junction" water tower, the last one standing in the state. Driving down Main Street, you half expect to see Uncle Joe and the rest of the cast from that zany comedy.

Drive through the town to see the water tower, but stop because of its train depot. Chuck Zobel has transformed the once bustling passenger station into the ◆ **Grant Depot Restaurant,** one of the county's best eateries—unless you're a railroad enthusiast, then it's a fascinating train museum that serves a very good Mile High Lemon (meringue) Pie.

After purchasing the empty depot in 1979, Zobel spent a year renovating, and in the process of tearing down walls and replacing floors, he turned up a variety of artifacts from the era of the iron horse: tickets and train orders from 1903, bottles, telegrams, signs, even the remains of a copper sulfate battery that powered the telegraph before the age of electricity. Today you can sit at a table in what a century ago was the passenger waiting room, or in a bay window overlooking the tracks, where a station agent once worked a telegraph. What was the baggage room is now the kitchen, and the dining room walls are covered with memorabilia—from lanterns and oil cans to warning lights, tickets, and an engineer's manual on how to operate a locomotive.

The Grant Depot Restaurant (616–834–7361) is open 7:30 A.M. to 8:00 P.M. Monday through Thursday, until 9:00 P.M. Friday and Saturday, and from 11:30 A.M. to 3:00 P.M. Sunday. From I–96 in Grand Rapids, head north on M–37 (exit 30). Grant is reached in 24 miles, and the Depot is right off M–37.

Wildflower lovers ought to stay on M–37 in Newaygo County to reach ◆ **Loda Lake Wildflower Sanctuary.** In 1938, Forest Service rangers invited the Federated Garden Clubs of Michigan to help them create a sanctuary for native plants, including endangered and protected species, to ensure their survival. Although part of the Manistee National Forest, the preserve is still managed by the Federated Garden Clubs, and over the years it has evolved into a unique haven for botanists, wildflower enthusiasts, and families who just want to know the difference between Michigan holly and Holly, Michigan.

The self-guiding trail is a mile loop of easy hiking where you encounter the first numbered post in less than 20 feet, and before you return to the picnic area, you'll pass thirty-nine posts. The interpretive posts mark the location of trillium, blueberries, swamp rose, insect-eating sundew plants, and fragrant water lily, among the other plants, and they correspond to a trail guide available near the parking area.

From White Cloud head north on M–37 and then left on Five Mile Road, where the directional sign to Loda Lake is posted on the corner. Head a mile west and turn right on Fletcher Road. The entrance to the sanctuary is a mile to the north. To obtain a trail guide, stop at the U.S. Forest Service Ranger Station on M–37 in White Cloud, which has an information parlor open twenty-four hours a day, or call (616) 689–6696.

LAKE COUNTY

When you look at a stump what do you see? A stump? Is a tree root just a tree root? Not to Ray Overholzer.

This hunting guide–turned–craftsman would stroll along the Pere Marquette River, find a stump leftover from Michigan's logging era, and see a table or maybe a piece of rocking chair. Then he would spend months fashioning it by hand until his unique vision became reality. This is woodworking as an art, and it's preserved today at ◆ **Shrine of the Pines,** a small but, to those of us who struggled in shop class just to build that birdhouse, an intriguing museum.

He constructed a rocking chair from roots that was so perfectly balanced it rocks fifty-five times with a single push. His gun rack holds twelve hunting rifles and rotates on hand-carved wooden balls like ball bearings. Not a screw or a hinge in the elaborate cabinet. A stump became a bootlegger's table with a hidden compartment for the whiskey bottle and another for the shot glasses. Perhaps most amazing is the dining room table that began as a 700-pound stump of a giant white pine. By the time Overholzer was done working with the piece of discarded wood, it was a 300-pound table with roots carved into legs and storage binds hollowed out of the sides.

Between 1940 and 1941 Overholzer built a huge lodge on the banks of the Pere Marquette and originally intended to operate it as a hunting lodge. But his furniture was too dear to him by then, and fearing it would get scratched, he changed his mind. The intended lodge became a museum of more than 200 pieces, the world's only collection of handcrafted white pine furniture.

The Shrine of the Pines (616–745–7892) is located on M–37, 2 miles south of Baldwin. The museum is open daily, May–October, 10:00 A.M.–6:00 P.M. There is a small fee.

OCEANA COUNTY

County Road B–15 departs from US–31 north of Whitehall and swings west toward the Lake Michigan shoreline before returning to the highway at Pentwater, the bustling resort community at the northwest corner of Oceana County. Along the way the county road passes Silver Lake, an impressive sight that slows most cars bearing sightseers to a crawl. The lake is bordered to the west by a huge dune that towers over it, and from the car window you see beach and sunbathers, crystal clear lake and sailboats, the mountain of sand and dune climbers. Much of what you see, including the strip of dunes that lies between the inland lake and Lake Michigan, is part of ◈ **Silver Lake State Park.**

Silver Lake is different from other state parks along Lake Michigan, because the dunes have been divided into three separate areas for three types of users. The region to the south is one of only two places in the state where dune rides are offered in large open-air jeeps that hold up to twelve passengers (**Mac Wood's Dune Rides,** 616–873–2817). The section in the middle is the pedestrian area, where people scramble up the huge dunes and hike across them to Lake Michigan.

The northern area of the park is most unusual as it is designated for off-road vehicles. This is the ORV capital of the Midwest, the only public dunes in Michigan where people can drive their three- and four-wheelers, dirt bikes, trail jeeps, or any other vehicle built for the soft sand and steep terrain. On almost any day of the summer, the ORV parking lot at the end of Hazel Road will be filled with a wide assortment of vehicles, their drivers, and the trailers and vans they arrived in. They come from Indiana, Illinois, Ohio, and Wisconsin to ride here, as well as from all over Michigan. Pedestrians don't venture into the motorized area, but there is a wooden viewing platform overlooking the ORV entry point. Here you can view all the daredevil drivers and their machines as they climb the first dune.

For the more adventurous, ◈ **Sandy Korners** offers guided drives on the dunes. Each person is given dune buggy, helmet, and instructions for safe usage. A guide then leads the group on a one- to two-hour run across the sandy hills. Sandy Korners (616–873–5048) is on Hazel Road before you enter the state park and charges $40 an hour for the rides. All participants must have a driver's license. There is a vehicle fee to enter Silver Lake State Park (616–873–3083).

MASON COUNTY

Continue on South Lakeshore Drive, pass the huge Ludington Power Plant, and then after a few miles keep an eye on the east side of the road for ◆ **Bortell's Fisheries.** From the outside the fish market is not glamorous, but it has been in business since 1937 and gradually has evolved into west Michigan's finest shop for fish and seafood. They carry a variety of frozen seafood, make delicious marinated herring in cream and wine, and smoke one of the best selections of fish in the state, including trout, chub, salmon, sturgeon, blind robin, and menominee. Want something fresher? When in season, their cases are filled with fresh perch, pike, walleye, trout, and even smelt in the spring, all half buried in ice.

Still not fresh enough? Then you can wander around back with a pole and catch a rainbow trout out of one of their stocked ponds. They will cook any fresh fish right there in the market and serve it with french fries and homemade potato salad or coleslaw. You can enjoy your meal outside at one of a half dozen picnic tables next to the market, or better yet cross the street to Summit Park, where you have a view of Lake Michigan from your table. The freshest fish, good food, and beautiful scenery at a little out-of-the-way county park—it doesn't get much better than that.

Bortell's Fisheries (616–843–3337) is 7 miles south of Ludington on South Lakeshore Drive between Meisenhiemer and Deren roads. From May through September the store is open daily from 11:00 A.M. until 8:00 P.M.

The first frame house in Mason County was built by Aaron Burr Caswell in 1849. Six years later the two-story home was still the only frame building in an area that was trying to organize itself into Michigan's newest county. So that year Caswell offered the front half of his home as the first courthouse and county seat of Mason. Today the preserved building is a state historic

Trapper's Cabin in White Pine Village

site and the centerpiece of ◆ **White Pine Village,** a museum complex operated by the Mason County Historical Society.

The village is composed of some twenty preserved buildings or replicas, all from the surrounding county and set up along streets on a bluff overlooking Lake Michigan. Each of the buildings, which range from an 1840s trapper's log cabin to a hardware store of the early 1900s, is completely renovated inside and can be viewed on a leisurely self-guided walk. Throughout the village people in traditional dress apply their trades, everything from a blacksmith, to a turn-of-the-century housewife cooking on a wood stove, to a violin maker.

What makes White Pine Village an enjoyable experience is the active visitor participation in the exhibits. A documented trial that was held in the Caswell home in the 1860s is reenacted today with visitors filling in as the jury and nine out of ten times handing down the same verdict as the first time. A log chapel on the rise overlooking the area still holds Sunday service, and afterward people are encouraged to help the village cooks and enjoy their fresh baked treats.

White Pine Village (616–843–4808) is open from Memorial Day until Labor Day Tuesday through Sunday from 11:00 A.M. to 4:30 P.M. The museum complex is located off US–31, 3 miles south of Ludington, and is reached by exiting west onto Iris Road and then turning north at South Lakeshore Drive for a quarter of a mile. There is a small admission fee.

From Ludington the famous dunes of Lake Michigan continue to the north, and the area immediately adjacent to the city has been preserved as Ludington State Park. It's a popular place where visitors enjoy miles of beach, rolling dunes, and modern campgrounds, or a hike to historic Point Sable Lighthouse. Where Ludington State Park ends, the ◆ **Nordhouse Dunes** begin, a 1,900-acre preserve in Manistee National Forest that is not as well known or visited as much as the state park but is equally beautiful.

A Michigan governor called the Nordhouse Dunes "one of the most outstanding scenic resources" in the state, and in 1987 they were given a federal wilderness designation. What makes these dunes unique is that the area is entirely undeveloped. Travel through the dunes is only on foot either along 10 miles of easy-to-follow trails or by simply making your way across the open hills of sand. The area is the only place in Michigan where you can hike in and camp among the dunes. Because of its inaccessibility to motorized traffic, the dunes area also offers the opportunity, for those willing to hike in, of having a beach to themselves along its 4 miles of sandy lakeshore.

Access into Nordhouse Dunes is through the Lake Michigan Recreation Area, a semiprimitive campground on the northern end of the preserve that is maintained by the Manistee Ranger District (616–723–2211) of the national forest. Trails into the dunes begin from the recreation area, which also contains one hundred camping sites, a beach, and observation towers overlooking the lake. To reach the recreational area, take US–31 to Lake Michigan Road (also known as Forest Road 5629) located 10 miles south of Manistee. Follow Lake Michigan Road 8 miles west to the area. There is no fee for exploring the dunes or for day use of the recreational area. There is a nightly fee for camping.

MANISTEE COUNTY

Manistee is another lakeshore town that boomed during the lumbering era; at one time in the late 1800s it boasted thirty-two sawmills and seventeen millionaire lumber barons among its residents. Almost the entire town was destroyed in the Great Fire of 1871 on the very day Chicago experienced one of its worse blazes. One of the first buildings erected after the fiery mishap was the Lyman Building, which was a place of business throughout its existence until the Manistee County Historical Society turned it into the only "storefront museum in the state."

◆ **The Lyman Building Museum** is not just another county museum displaying local artifacts. The many fixtures, walk-in vault, and wraparound balcony have been preserved, and part of the first floor has been restored as an early drugstore with brass apothecary scales, pill makers, an impressive selection of antique medicines and balms, and fading posters on the walls selling Pe-Ru-Na, which "cures catarrh." The other half of the first floor is set up as a general store, while in the back is an old newspaper office with original Linotype machines.

Upstairs are ten more rooms, including a dentist's office, a bank, and the living room of an early 1900s home. The hallway between the rooms is filled with Victor talking machines and Victrolas. The Lyman Building Museum (616–723–5531), at 425 River Street in downtown Manistee, is open year-round from 10:00 A.M. to 5:00 P.M. Monday through Saturday from June through September and Tuesday through Saturday the rest of the year. There is a small admission charge.

Another impressive building left over from the town's golden lumbering era is the ◆ **Ramsdell Theatre,** built in 1903 by Thomas Jefferson Ramsdell and today listed on the National Register of Historic Places. Ramsdell, a local lawyer and later a state legislator, wanted to add some culture to the rough-and-

99

tumble logging town and built one of the most elaborate opera houses in the state. It featured a double balcony upstairs and private viewing boxes along the main floor. It was proclaimed "acoustically perfect," and famed theatrical artist Walter Burridge painted the main curtain, which is still used today. Other paintings adorn the dome and archways of the lobby.

Citizens saved the theater from demolition in the 1920s, and the city finally purchased the structure in 1943. Today the Manistee Civic Players operate the facility and use it to stage a summer series of plays. Stop in when the box office is open (a week before each show, Monday through Saturday from noon to 6:00 P.M.) and you can view the interior. Or call (616–723–9948) for a tour of the opera house. Ramsdell Theatre is on First and Maple streets.

Northern Michigan is famous for its trout streams, which attract fly fishermen from around the country. In Manistee County, you can either grab your fly rod and go fishing or go to school to learn how to fly fish. The ❖**Michigan Academy of Fly Fishing** is part of Wellston Inn and is located near some of the state's best blue-ribbon trout streams, in the small town of Wellston. Five times each summer the academy holds a two- or three-day class, with students staying at the historical Wellston Inn. Not only does the inn provide a comfortable room, but outside there is a lighted fly-casting pond and a fly-tying hut.

Students divide their time between the inn's facilities and local rivers, learning how to work a fly rod, read trout waters, choose a fly, and even tie their own. The three-day sessions are $400 per person and include rooms. For reservations or dates write The Wellston Inn, P.O. Box 70, Wellston 49689, or call (616) 848–4163.

NORTHWEST MICHIGAN

1. Gwen Frostic Prints
2. Northwest Soaring Club of Frankfort
3. Platte River Point
4. Homestead Sugar House
5. Sugar Shack
6. Sleeping Bear Point Coast Guard Station Maritime Museum
7. South Manitou Island
8. Boskydel Vineyard
9. *Malabar*
10. Grand Traverse Balloon
11. Château Chantal Vineyard
12. The Music House
13. Amon Orchards
14. Deadman's Hill
15. Fisherman's Island State Park
16. Beaver Island
17. Horton Bay General Store
18. Ironton Ferry
19. Fonds du Cuisine Cooking School
20. Little Traverse Historical Museum
21. Legs Inn
22. Cheboygan County Historical Museum
23. Mill Creek Historical State Park
24. Pigeon River Country State Forest
25. Hartwick Pines State Park
26. Civilian Conservation Corps Museum
27. Carl T. Johnson Hunting and Fishing Center

NORTHWEST MICHIGAN

In many ways Northwest Michigan is a continuation of the region stretching along Lake Michigan. It's accented by vast tracts of dunes, miles of beaches, and a handful of well-developed resort towns whose specialty shops bustle in the summer and winter. But it is also distinctly different.

This is "the land of many little bays," with scenic Grand Traverse Bay dominating the center of the region, Little Traverse Bay farther up the shoreline, and remote Sturgeon Bay at its northern tip. For many tourists this is Mackinaw City, a tour of Fort Michilimackinac, and a ferry ride to Mackinac Island, the summer resort island known throughout the country for its horse-and-carriage transportation and the Grand Hotel.

Most of all, this is Michigan's Cherry Country. Moderate weather from the Great Lakes and light soils help this region produce 80 to 85 percent of the state's total cherry crop. Drive along US–31 from Traverse City to Charlevoix in spring, and you'll pass rolling hills of trees in full bloom and air scented by cherry blossoms.

Arrive in July and you can enjoy the bountiful harvest these fruit farms produce. Along this 50-mile stretch of road, you'll pass dozens of farms and will undoubtedly see harvesting crews "shaking" one tree after another, with the cherries ending up in a large metal tank of water.

You'll also see numerous roadside fruit stands that will be hard to pass up, and you shouldn't even try. The most common sweet cherries sold are Bing and Schmidt; tourists often call them black cherries, though if they are, the fruit is overripe. Look for cherries that are firm and dark maroon, and be prepared when you bite into your first one. The juice will explode from the cherry, dribble down your chin, and send your taste buds into a state of ecstasy. There are few things as wonderful in this state as a northern Michigan cherry in July.

BENZIE COUNTY

One of the smallest counties in the state, Benzie is also one of the most scenic. It features rolling forested hills, spring-fed trout streams, towering sandy bluffs, and endless beaches along Lake

Michigan and Crystal Lake, a body of water whose clarity lives up to its name. In the natural beauty of this northwoods setting, Gwen Frostic emerged as one of Michigan's most noted poets and publishers from her background as an artist and a conservationist. Her love of nature has always been with her, but she began writing and carving blocks for prints in the mid-1940s in the blue-collar community of Wyandotte, located south of Detroit. In the early 1960s she moved to a wooded spot 2 miles west of Benzonia and set up ◆ **Gwen Frostic Prints** on a personal wildlife sanctuary of 285 acres.

Her large gallery is housed in a building of native stone, glass, and old wood, which seeks to "bring the outdoors in" while blending into the natural surroundings. She accomplished that surprisingly well. Inside you'll walk below rough-cut beams past huge stone fireplaces and view the tumbling water of natural fountains. You'll be surrounded by Frostic's woodblock prints, tables covered with books of her poetry, and bird carvings by some of the country's leading wildlife carvers. There is a small library overlooking a pond where waterfowl usually are feeding, and another room displays all the honors she has received, including the proclamation of an official "Gwen Frostic Day" set aside by a Michigan governor.

Most impressive, perhaps, is the publishing aspect of the gallery. From a balcony above, visitors can view fifteen original Heidelberg presses clanking away as workers print a wide selection of cards, notepaper, wall prints, and books, all using block designs carved by Frostic, featuring natural subjects and sold in the gallery. The artist/poet is now in her eighties and lives on the top floor of the gallery, but she regularly comes down to meet her patrons and autograph copies of her books.

Gwen Frostic Prints (616–882–5505) is at 5140 River Road, 2 miles west of US–31 and 6 miles east of M–22 in Frankfort. The gallery is open daily from May to October from 9:00 A.M. until 5:30 P.M. and until 4:30 P.M. Monday through Saturday the rest of the year. The presses are in operation only Monday through Friday.

Back in the 1930s, a small group of Frankfort residents discovered the thrill of soaring in gliders. They would take off from the high bluffs overlooking Lake Michigan and soar through the air, sometimes for hours, before landing on the beach. What emerged was the ◆ **Northwest Soaring Club of Frankfort,** which at one time hosted a national soaring championship in this small town.

The art of soaring has changed over the years, but the club is still around, offering lessons and, for visitors passing through on vacation, introductory rides. Passengers join a certified pilot in a two-seat glider that measures 25 to 35 feet in length, with a wingspan of around 50 feet. The glider is towed 2,000 to 3,000 feet in the air by a small plane and then released. What follows is a spectacular ride along the Lake Michigan shoreline with extensive views of the lake, sand dunes, and beautiful Crystal Lake. The length of the ride depends on the wind and thermal conditions of the day, but it ranges from thirty minutes to sometimes several hours.

Introductory rides are offered from May through October and cost $30 per person. Interested persons should call ahead to the Northwest Soaring Club at (616) 352–9160. The club now takes off from Frankfort Airport, located on Airport Road, south of M–115.

Of all the dunes along Lake Michigan, the best known within the state and around the country are those in Sleeping Bear National Lakeshore, administered by the National Park Service. Thousands visit the area every year, and many head straight to the **"Dune Climb,"** a 150-foot steep hill of sand located right off M–109 in Leelanau County. This is the park's most famous feature, a knee-bending climb up the towering dune and a wild run down through the soft sand. In addition, there are other aspects of the park, many having nothing to do with dunes and often overlooked by visitors who rush through the area in an afternoon.

The national lakeshore begins in Benzie County and includes one of the most scenic beaches on Lake Michigan. ◆ **Platte River Point** is a long, sandy spit divided from the mainland by the crystal-clear Platte River. It's pure sand, this narrow strip, with endless Lake Michigan on one side, the knee-deep salmon and trout river on the other, and panoramas of towering dunes off in the distance. To reach it, sunbathers turn west from M–22 onto the marked Lake Michigan Road and follow it to its end. Then it's a quick wade through the rippling waters of the Platte River with Dad holding young ones or the picnic lunch high on his shoulder. There is no bridge.

People at Platte River Point swim, build sand castles, and beachcomb as on any other beach, but the favorite activity here is floating. They bring out an old inner tube or an air mattress, hike a few hundred yards up the point, and then allow the Platte River to give them a free ride right out to Lake Michigan if they wish. It's debatable who enjoys it more, the kids or the parents. If you don't have an inner tube, you can rent one from **Riverside Canoe Trips** (616–325–5622) located on M–22 right before you turn off for the beach. They rent tubes for one to four persons and even have dropoff and pickup services for those who want to spend an afternoon "tubing" the Platte River from the Platte Lake to the Great Lake. Rental rates vary depending on the length of your float and the size of your tube.

The sign out front says all you need to know about the ◆**Homestead Sugar House.** It's attached to a wooden scaffold, located just below the large noose and reads HANG THE DIET! Don't even think about "that four-letter word" when you stumble upon the maple bush of Jean and Russell Morstadt, home of Benzie County's oldest candymaking shop. Don't worry about counting calories or losing that 2-inch pinch at the waist. Just enjoy the aroma that greets you as soon as you pull in; let your eyes feast on the hand-dipped, long-stemmed chocolate cherries and maple creams displayed in the glass case inside; and when Jean Morstadt, dressed in a Grandma Moses motif, offers you something sweet, don't be bashful.

The Morstadts were living in Chicago in 1948, when they decided they had had enough of city life, and they moved to northern Michigan. They bought a 300-acre maple bush in the rolling hills east of Beulah and began farming. After years of "harvesting nothing but bills," the couple began making candy in the shack outside their home in 1963. They recently celebrated their thirtieth anniversary as candymakers, and among their loyal customers is singer Linda Ronstadt.

From US–31 turn onto Homestead Road in downtown Benzonia and head east for 4.5 miles to the farm with a scaffold on the outside. The shop (616–882–7712) is open from 9:30 A.M. to 5:00 P.M. daily May through November.

LEELANAU COUNTY

If it's March and you have a sweet tooth, head north to Maple City, where you'll find the ◆**Sugar Shack,** a 200-acre, 900-tree sugar maple bush. In northern Michigan, the season can last up to six weeks and usually begins in mid-March, when the freezing and thawing cycle of spring causes the sap to flow. The season is not long, but it's a special time, and visitors can witness it by stopping in at this farm set in the rolling, wooded hills south of Glen Lake.

A visit to this bush is a view of a modern-day maple producer, and most people interested in the process begin with a walk into the bush to see a pumping station and the network of tubing. Others never leave the small store with its potbellied stove and rustic appearance. Shelves are stocked with maple sugar by the pound and by the piece, homemade maple pralines, maple-coated popcorn, and, of course, syrup.

The Sugar Shack (616–228–5835) is located just off M–72, 15 miles west of Traverse City. From M–72 turn north on Fritz Road and in a quarter of a mile turn west on Baatz Road, from where the farm is 1.5 miles on the left. During the syrup season and the summer, the store is open 9:00 A.M. to 5:00 P.M. Monday through Friday and until noon on Saturday.

For a view of spectacular dune terrain, take a ride along the **Pierce Stocking Scenic Drive** at Sleeping Bear National Lakeshore. This is one of the main attractions of the area today. At the turn of the century, however, the noted feature was the Manitou Passage, which lies between the Manitou Islands and the mainland. During the heyday of Great Lake shipping from the 1860s to 1920, when on a single day a hundred vessels might pass through, this was a shoal-lined shortcut they all followed. Manitou Passage's shallow reeflike shoals, narrow passage, and often violent weather produced more than its share of shipwrecks, and eventually several lighthouses and lifesaving stations were built on the mainland and the islands.

One of them has been preserved by the National Park Service as ◆ **Sleeping Bear Point Coast Guard Station Maritime Museum.** The facility began its service in 1901 as a U.S. Life Saving Station and was actually situated on Sleeping Bear Point. When, in 1930, a migrating sand dune threatened to bury it, the U.S. Coast Guard (having replaced the U.S. Life Saving Service) moved the buildings 1.5 miles toward Glen Haven. The station ended its duty in 1942 and now is a well-restored museum that tells the story of the U.S. Life Saving Service, which manned the coastline all around the country.

Anywhere from six to ten men would live at the remote station, and their former living quarters, a huge two-story building, is now the main exhibit area. It allows visitors a glimpse of the regimented work they performed and the isolated life they lived. Nearby the boathouse contains the lifesaving boats, complete with tracks down to the beach for a quick launching, and other equipment, including the beachcart. When ships ran aground within 400 yards of shore, the lifesavers would pull out the beachcart and use the small cannon on it to shoot a guide line onto the distressed vessel. That rope was used to string more lines across the water, and a "breeches buoy" was sent to the ship on a pulley. Then one by one sailors would step into the breeches of the buoy and ride the line to the shore and safety.

Check with the park headquarters (616–326–5134) in Empire for time and day of the museum's "Heroes of the Storm" program, when rangers demonstrate a turn-of-the-century shipwreck rescue using the beachcart, the breeches buoy, and volunteers from the audience who fill in for sailors and lifesavers. Only the cannon is missing.

The village of Leland's trademark is a row of weathered dockside shacks along the Leland River that at one time housed commercial fishermen and today is a historic district known as Fishtown. All the commercial fishermen except Carlson Fisheries have disappeared from the strip, but their buildings have been preserved and now house specialty shops and stores. With its unique setting and atmosphere, Fishtown is the proper place to begin a nautical adventure to ❖ **South Manitou Island,** a portion of the Sleeping Bear National Lakeshore located 17 miles from Leland in Lake Michigan.

Island visitors board a ferry at the end of Fishtown and begin with a ninety-minute cruise to South Manitou that passes a lighthouse and the scenic shoreline of Sleeping Bear Dunes. The island, with its hardwood forests and natural harbor, attracted settlers, a lighthouse, and a lifesaving station as early as 1840, and it possesses an interesting history. The ferry has a four-hour layover at the national park dock, more than enough time to view the small museum at the visitor's center, climb the 116 steps to the top of the lighthouse, and enjoy a lunch on the nearby beaches.

For the more energetic, there are trails and old farms roads across the island, and it's possible to hike the 6-mile round trip to the

Francisco Morazan and return to the mainland the same day. The *Morazan* was a Liberian freighter that ran aground in November 1960, in the southwest corner of the island, and a large portion of the battered vessel is still visible above the waterline today. For the best adventure on South Manitou, camp for a night or two at Weather Station Campground, a national park facility that is free. The campground is a 1.5-mile hike in from the dock, and you can explore the tract of sand dunes on the west side of the island. The dunes, perched high above Lake Michigan on bluffs, are probably the most remote and least visited ones in Michigan.

All visitors must bring their own food to South Manitou, and campers have to be self-sufficient with tent, sleeping bags, and other equipment. Contact Manitou Island Transit (616–256–9061 or 271–4217) regarding the ferry that sails for the island daily June through August. Round-trip fares range from $13 to $18.

The growing conditions in southwest Michigan that made Paw Paw the wine-producing center of the state are also found in Leelanau and Old Missionary, two peninsulas filled with fruit farms and a half dozen vineyards of surprising quality. All the vineyards have a tasting room, and an interesting day can be had visiting each one of them. The first bonded wine cellar in the area—and many think the most beautiful one in the state—is ◈ **Boskydel Vineyard,** a small winery on the shores of Lake Leelanau. There is no restaurant at Boskydel or even any picnic tables outside, but it is built on the side of a hill, and from the parking lot you have a view of the sloping vineyard leading down to the huge lake, framed by the rolling hills of the Leelanau Peninsula. All this prompted one wine critic to proclaim Boskydel the most beautiful site for a winery in the country.

It was within the family tradition that Bernie Rinke should plant a vineyard. He grew up on an Ohio farm, and his father bootlegged wine during Prohibition. Rinke began planting his vineyard in 1964 and now cultivates twenty-five acres of grapes, producing 6,000 gallons (2,500 cases) annually of several dry and semi-dry red and white table wines. The tasting room is open daily year-round from 1:00 to 6:00 P.M., and if you want a tour of the winery, Rinke will lead you through a ten-minute look at his facility.

Actually, Rinke would rather stay in the small tasting room, plop a large wine glass in front of you (no plastic cups here), and talk . . . about his grapes, about wine tasting, about his days as Northwestern Michigan College's first librarian in nearby Traverse City (ask him where the name of the winery comes from). A beautiful vineyard, a most delightful winemaker, and not a bad wine either. Boskydel (616–256–7272) is 3.5 miles southeast of the town of Lake Leelanau on the corner of County Road 641 and Otto Road.

GRAND TRAVERSE COUNTY

The most noted feature of the county is Grand Traverse Bay, a beautiful body of water that is outlined by Traverse City to the south and split up the middle by Mission Peninsula. Its protected waters have become a haven for sailboats, catamarans, and sailboarders, but by far the most impressive vessel afloat during the summer is the ❖ *Malabar,* an 1850 replica of a two-masted, gaff-rigged, topsail schooner. The 105-foot, 100-ton ship was built in 1975 in Bath, Maine, and splits its sailing days with summers in Traverse City and winters in Key West.

It is built to look and sail like a traditional schooner, and it's that love for old wooden boats that draws most of its passengers on deck. From May to mid-October the *Malabar* offers three sailings daily, with two-hour cruises at noon and 3:00 P.M. and a two-and-a-half-hour sunset sail with picnic meal—the most popular trip, of course—at 7:00 P.M. Those passengers who dream about a life on the high seas go a step further and book a cabin on the *Malabar,* which at night becomes Michigan's only floating bed and breakfast. The quarters are tiny, with bunks built into the curves and angles of the hull. The head is shared, and the showers are back on land. In the evening guests wander topside to take in Traverse City lights shimmering on the bay or snuggle up in their bunks to be put to sleep by the gentle swells and the creaking of a wooden hull.

The *Malabar* is operated by Traverse Tall Ship Company (616–941–2000). Its office and dock are at 13390 Southwest Bay Shore Drive. Daily cruises range from $28 to $38 for adults, and overnight accommodations, which include a hearty breakfast with the crew in the galley, are $95 to $175 for singles or doubles.

You can also enjoy the water from above through ❖ **Grand Traverse Balloon,** which offers hot-air balloon tours across

109

The *Malabar*

Grand Traverse Bay, often beginning in the Château Grand Traverse vineyards on Old Missionary Peninsula. This may well be the most spectacular view from any hot-air balloon in Michigan, as below you lies the narrow peninsula, the rippling waters of the bay, Traverse City, and the endless rows of the cherry orchards to the northeast. The entire flight takes three hours, with an hour in the air, and flights are always held at sunrise or sunset (less wind turbulence). They are priced at $165 per person. Jeff Geiger, the Traverse City balloonist who runs Grand Traverse Balloon (616–947–RIDE), recommends reservations but says he can usually fulfill last-minute urges to float above the bay.

For another unusual view of the bay, head to the highest ridge along Mission Peninsula just before sunset. At this high point Robert Begin has built the state's newest vineyard, ◆ **Château Chantal,** and included a brick terrace that overlooks not just the West Arm or the East Arm of Grand Traverse Bay but both of them. With vineyards and cherry orchards at your feet, you settle back with a glass of Chardonnay or a semi-dry Riesling and some sharp cheeses or freshly cut fruit and watch the sky melt into a collage of oranges and reds over the bays of Northern Michigan.

Begin, a former priest, and his wife have built the unique winery on a former ridge-top cherry farm and named the winery after their daughter. You can stop by for a tour or a sip in the vineyard's wine-tasting and sales area, a great room in the château that features hardwood floors, a polished granite bar top, and a grand piano in front of a 20-foot-wide bay window overlooking Grand Traverse Bay.

You can also stop for a sunset, stop for jazz on Thursday evenings, or you can simply stop for the night and unwind. That's because this winery is also a bed and breakfast, featuring three rooms with sitting areas and private baths.

Château Chantal (616–223–4110) is located just off M–37 on Mission Peninsula, 12 miles north of Traverse City. Sunsets on the terrace are Monday through Saturday 6:00 P.M. to 9:00 P.M., June through September, with special Jazz at Sunsets on Thursday evenings in July and August. Tours are offered daily 11:00 A.M. to 6:00 P.M. and noon to 5:00 P.M. on Sunday. Rooms range from $85 to $115 per night.

If you're traveling just north of Traverse City on US–31 and pass a place called ◆ **The Music House,** turn off the car stereo.

111

Strip the headphones and Walkmans from your kids' ears and toss that huge boom box in the trunk. Then turn around and see how music used to be enjoyed. Housed in an old granary built in 1905, The Music House is a showcase for automatic musical instruments from the 1880s to the 1920s. Visitors are entertained rather than educated, as the hour-long tour is a musical journey with toe-tapping demonstrations ranging from small music boxes to one of the largest ballroom dance organs ever made.

Tours begin in the phonograph gallery, where a huge model of Nipper, the famous RCA Victor dog, greets you. There are rows of "talking machines" beginning from 1900 with their wax cylinders instead of records and colorful morning glory horns instead of speakers. In the main portion of the barn are larger musical machines set up in the environments in which they were enjoyed. The most impressive sight for many visitors is upstairs in the loft of the barn, which is home to the 30-foot facade of the Amaryllis dance organ. Built in 1922 for a palace ballroom in Belgium, the instrument plays a folded perforated cardboard book using hundreds of wooden and metal pipes along with percussion instruments.

The Music House (616–938–9300) is located on a 180-acre cherry farm off US–31, 1.5 miles north of the highway's junction with M–72 or 8 miles north of Traverse City. The attraction is open from "cherry blossoms through fall colors," or to be more exact, May 1 through October 30, 10:00 A.M. to 4:00 P.M. Monday through Saturday and 1:00 to 5:00 P.M. on Sunday. There is an admission fee.

Continue north on US–31 for a few more miles and you'll come to ◆**Amon Orchards,** offering guided tours and the best view of a working cherry farm. Visitors ride in an open tractor trolley, and in July you can watch workers mechanically harvest cherries and even pick a few of your own. Tours at Amon Orchards (616–938–1644), beginning in July and continuing through September, are offered at 10:00 A.M. and 2:00 P.M. daily. There is a fee for the ninety-minute tour.

ANTRIM COUNTY

Speeding along US–131 in the middle of Antrim County, you pass one of the most spectacular inland viewing points in the

Lower Peninsula, though you would never know it from this road. The side road to ◆**Deadman's Hill** is 7 miles north of Mancelona, but there is little fanfare about the scenic overlook: Only a small brown sign points the way. Follow Deadman's Hill Road for 1.5 miles until it dead-ends at a pair of Department of Natural Resources pit toilets and a wood-chip path. Some 15 yards up the path is a spectacular panorama from the high point of more than 1,200 feet. You take in a 180-degree view of the Jordan River valley stretching 15 miles to rugged hills that fill the horizon. During October the view from this spot is priceless, as the entire valley with the winding river through it is on fire with autumn reds and oranges.

Deadman's Hill earned its name from the logging era at the turn of the century. The steep hills made the Jordan River valley a treacherous place to log, and numerous accidents occurred. But people grieved the most in 1910 when "Big Sam" Graczyk, twenty-one years old and soon to be married, was killed while driving a team of horses and a big wheel of logs. The name for the ridge stuck. You can admire the view, have a picnic while sitting on the edge, and the more adventurous can hike the Jordan River Pathway, which begins at this point. Part of the trail is a 3-mile loop down to the river and back, or it can be turned into an 18-mile overnight walk to a hike-in campground for backpackers.

CHARLEVOIX COUNTY

South of Charlevoix off US–31 is yet another state park along Lake Michigan. ◆**Fisherman's Island State Park** possesses many of the same features as the other parks: 3 miles of sandy shoreline, excellent swimming areas, some scenic views of the Great Lake. But Fisherman's Island also has a couple of unique features. Not nearly as popular or crowded, the park offers fifteen rustic campsites right on Lake Michigan. Each one is tucked away in the trees with a table and a spot to pitch a tent only a few feet from the lapping waters of the lake. These are some of the most beautiful campsites in the Lower Peninsula, and naturally they are the first to be chosen in the campground. Be prepared to camp on an island site the first night and then claim a lakeside one first thing the next morning.

The other noted feature of the state park is the Petoskey stones. The state stone is actually petrified coral, a leftover fragment of the many coral reefs that existed in the warm-water seas from Charlevoix to Alpena some 300 million years ago. Today the stones are collected by rock hounds, and many of them end up polished and used in jewelry, paperweights, and other decorative items. Dry stones are silvery with no apparent markings to the untrained eye, but when the rocks are wet it's easy to see the ringlike pattern that covers them. Rock hounds searching for the stones are usually seen closely inspecting the waterline or washing off handfuls of rocks in the lake.

The 2.5-mile park road begins at the ranger station and ends at the sandy beaches of the state park but along the way passes an extended rocky shoreline. Many gem enthusiasts say this is one of the best places in northern Michigan to find Petoskey stones. Stop at the ranger station for a park map and handout on the famous stones. There is a vehicle fee to enter Fisherman's Island State Park (616–547–6641) and an additional charge to camp overnight.

The Great Lakes that have blessed Michigan with miles of magnificent shoreline also have given it many islands that have become unique destinations for visitors. The most popular is Mackinac Island, a non-motorized resort (no cars or buses) that tourists flock to each summer, taking ferries out of Mackinaw City in the Lower Peninsula or St. Ignace across the Mackinac Bridge on the Upper Peninsula. There are also many islands without the crowds, commercialization, and fudge shops of Mackinac that make for an interesting side trip. One of the largest is ◆ **Beaver Island**, reached by a ferry from Charlevoix.

Known as "Emerald Isle" for its strong Irish heritage, Beaver Island lies 32 miles northwest of Charlevoix and is 55 square miles of forests, inland lakes, and farms. Its recorded history dates back to 1832, when Bishop Frederic Baraga, the Snowshoe Priest, brought Christianity to a small Indian settlement here. The island's most bizarre period began in 1847 after James Jesse Strang arrived. Strang and his band of Mormon followers had just broken away from the leadership of Brigham Young and established St. James, the island's only village. Eventually Strang would crown himself "King of Beaver Island" and rule the island and its religious sect with an iron hand before being shot in 1856 by a disgruntled subject. Irish immigrants followed in the 1870s to fish the waters of northern Lake Michigan, and today many of the 350 people who live year-round in or near St. James have roots back in Ireland.

Beaver Island has an assortment of lodge and hotel accommodations and restaurants for overnight visitors, but on Saturdays in July and August it also makes an ideal day trip. You can depart from Charlevoix at 8:30 A.M. on the ferry and reach the island by 11:00 A.M. for a six-hour visit before catching the last ferry back to the mainland at 5:30 P.M. In St. James there are two museums: the **Old Mormon Print Shop,** which was built by King Strang in 1850, and the **Marine and Harbor Museum,** a 1906 net shed dedicated to the time when the area bustled with fishermen.

You can also rent a mountain bike or a jeep and tour the island, which has more than a hundred miles of roads, most of them dirt and gravel. On a pleasant summer day, this is a most delightful adventure and a great way to see the old farmhouses, inland lakes, remote shoreline, and lighthouse located outside St. James. Pack a picnic lunch and plan on motoring three to four hours to circle Beaver Island. Beaver Island Boat Co. (616–547–2311) operates the ferry and charges $28 for a round-trip adult ticket. Beaver Island Sports and Rental (616–448–2266) in St. James rents mountain bikes and jeeps. For a complete list of island businesses, lodging, and sites, contact Beaver Island Chamber of Commerce, P.O. Box 5, Beaver Island, St. James 49781, (616) 448–2505.

A number of writers have ties to Northwest Michigan but none as famous as Ernest Hemingway, who spent the summers of his youth at his family's cottage on Walloon Lake. Hemingway buffs often tour the area to view artifacts and places that made their way into his writing. Most begin in Petoskey's Little Traverse Historical Museum (see Emmet County) and then head down US–141 past Walloon Lake. Some go to Hemingway Point on the south shore of Lake Charlevoix, where the young author once fled (it was owned by his uncle) when being pursued by a game warden. Of course, almost all eventually stop at the ◆ **Horton Bay General Store,** located across the lake on Boyne City Road.

Built in 1876 with a high false front, the store's most prominent feature is its large front porch with benches and stairs at either end. Hemingway idled away some youthful summers on that porch and fished nearby Horton Creek for rainbow and brook trout. He also celebrated his first marriage in Horton Bay's Congregational Church, and eventually the general store appeared in the opening of his short story "Up in Michigan." The Horton Bay General Store has had a string of owners, but remarkably little has changed about its appearance. It is still the classic general store; only the bright red benches outside receive a new coat of paint every now and then.

You enter through a flimsy screen door with a bell above it, and inside you find the worn wooden floors and shelves stacked with canned goods and other merchandise. There is an old wooden tub filled with ice and cold drinks, a small freezer that holds four or five flavors of ice cream, and the lunch counter where the morning coffee drinkers gather. Then as your eyes wander toward the ceiling, you realize this is more a preserved shrine to Hemingway than a store for the local residents. On one wall hang guns, old traps, mounted deer heads, and a panel of photographs of the author during his days in Northwest Michigan. Horton Bay General Store is open from 8:00 A.M. to 9:00 P.M. Monday through Saturday and until 5:00 P.M. on Sunday.

From Horton Bay you can continue around Lake Charlevoix in a scenic drive that will take you past Young State Park, through the historic downtown area of Boyne City, and near Hemingway Point, where Ferry Road abruptly ends at the South Arm of the lake. If you want to continue, you have to take passage on the ♟ **Ironton Ferry,** one of Michigan's most delightful boat rides even though it's only five minutes long.

Ferry service on the South Arm dates back to 1876, when the first barge was pulled back and forth by horses. It was apparently a money maker right from the start, as the 1884 rates are still listed on the side of the ferry office. The present ferry was installed in 1926 and is guided by cables 35 feet down on the lake bottom, making it, say officials, one of two cabled-operated automobile ferries in the country.

That's only one of the Ironton Ferry's many little oddities, the reason it was once featured in "Ripley's Believe It or Not." Consider its size (so small it holds only four cars), the length of its trip (a mere 575 feet of water), and the fact that it doesn't have a rudder. Perhaps most unusual is that the Ironton Ferry doesn't make regularly scheduled crossings. It's operated on demand because the South Arm is so narrow that passengers can be seen waiting on the other side.

The ferry operates from mid-April to Thanksgiving Eve 6:30 A.M. to 10:30 P.M. daily. A trip across is $1.50 per vehicle or 50 cents for walkers.

On the shores where Hemingway's family had their cottage are a number of historical buildings, including the Walloon Lake Inn. The century-old inn has a number of rooms upstairs, a fine lakeside restaurant downstairs, where you can arrive by car or boat, and, during the winter, the ◆ **Fonds du Cuisine Cooking School.** For four days small groups of students spend their mornings in the restaurant's kitchen working with chef David Beier and their afternoons in the dining room eating lunch. From Tuesday through Friday they are up to their elbows in sauces and batters at a school where textbooks are replaced by mixing bowls and wire whisks.

Classes are held between the countertop and the range, as the students receive their own ducks to truss and rainbow trout to fillet. Class ends with the midday meal, a lavish affair that may last two hours and usually involves a little wine tasting and comparing of each other's creations. Walloon Lake Inn (616–535–2999), in the heart of Walloon Lake Village, is 8 miles south of Petoskey and is reached from US–31 by heading west a quarter of a mile on M–75. The school is offered a dozen times September through mid-March and costs $400 per person, which includes four nights of lodging, breakfast, and daily luncheon.

EMMET COUNTY

Housed in Petoskey's Chicago and West Michigan railroad depot, which was built in 1892, the ◆ **Little Traverse Historical Museum** is the first logical stop on any Hemingway tour. The display case is small but contains photographs, other memorabilia, and some rare first-edition books that Hemingway autographed for his friend Edwin Pailthrorp, whom he visited in Petoskey in 1947. There is also a display case devoted to another famous writer, Bruce Catton, who was born in the Emmet County town and grew up in nearby Benzonia. Later Catton would pen *A Stillness at Appomattox*, for which he won a Pulitzer Prize in 1953. The original manuscript of that book and other

Little Traverse Historical Museum

personal artifacts now are in the museum.

The museum (616–347–2620) is on Dock Street on Petoskey's picturesque waterfront and is open April through October from 9:00 A.M. until 4:30 P.M. Monday through Saturday. There is a small admission fee.

From the well-developed resort town of Harbor Springs, M–119 heads north and hugs the coastline for 31 miles until it ends at Cross Village. It is often cited as a scenic drive, but not for the views of Lake Michigan you might expect when tracing it on a map. This is the **"Tunnel of Trees" Shore Drive,** a narrow road that climbs, drops, and curves its way through the thick forests along the rugged coast. At times the branches from trees at each side of the road merge overhead to form a complete tunnel, shading travelers even when the sun is beaming down at midday.

You finally emerge from the thick forest at Cross Village, a small hamlet and home of ✦ **Legs Inn.**

The inn is the creation of one man, Stanley Smolak, a Polish immigrant who fell in love with this part of Michigan and moved here from Chicago in 1921. Smolak quickly made friends with the local Ottawa Indians, who inducted him into their tribe as "Chief White Cloud." Then in 1930, with a Polish past, a love for northern Michigan, and his new Indian heritage, Smolak began building the inn. He combined the driftwood and stones he found along the shoreline to construct an unusual building on a bluff overlooking Lake Michigan. From the outside the architecture of the Legs Inn is bizarre, at best, but the interior is even more fascinating, for Smolak loved to carve the driftwood. He would take a piece, see something in it, and then whittle away. The inn has several rooms, all filled with Smolak's driftwood sculpture.

Naturally, the menu reflects Smolak's homeland and includes entrees of pierogi, gotabki, and bigos, a hearty Polish stew. They even serve a beer imported from Poland. The Legs Inn (616–526–2281) is located in the heart of Cross Village (you'll know it when you see it) and is open May through October from 11:00 A.M. until 10:00 P.M. and even later on Friday and Saturday. Dinner entrees on the menu range from $9.00 to $13.00.

CHEBOYGAN COUNTY

The residents are certainly friendly in Cheboygan. Arrive in this Lake Huron town of 5,100 from June to September, and the first place people want you to go is the jail. Stay as long as you like, they say. Plan to spend a few minutes in each cell, because that's where you'll find the pride and heritage that is Cheboygan—in the ✦ **Cheboygan County Historical Museum** located in the old county jail. At this museum you not only get to view the history of the area in an interesting series of displays and exhibits, you also have the opportunity to wander through a nineteenth-century jail. It's debatable which is more fascinating.

Built in 1890, the facility served as the area jail until 1970, when the county board of commissioners gave the building to the historical society. You enter the attached brick home where the county sheriff and his family lived, and the first room you walk into is a huge kitchen, where his wife cooked, not only for him and his family but for all the prisoners as well. From the home you pass through a metal door, entering the jail. Little has changed about the facility except that the historical society has filled each cell with a display, ranging from the town's first hardware stores to its maritime history to an exhibit on logging. Call it "history behind bars."

The museum is on the corner of Huron and Court streets. From US–23 within town, head south on M–27 and then west on Court Street for 3 blocks. The jail is open from June through Labor Day 1:00 to 3:00 P.M. Monday through Friday.

Another intriguing historical spot in Cheboygan County is just a few miles north on US–23. ◆**Mill Creek Historical State Park** was opened in 1984 after the site was "rediscovered" in 1972 by a local archaeologist. It dates back to the 1780s, when a Scottish trader named Robert Campbell obtained a 640-acre tract of land around the only stream in the area that had enough power to operate a mill, making the creek one of the oldest industrial centers in the Midwest. There was a great demand for lumber at the time, since the British were in the process of moving their military post from Fort Michilimackinac at the tip of the Lower Peninsula to Mackinac Island. The island's high limestone bluffs made it easier to defend against the Americans, who were thought to be on their way.

Visitors enter the area through an orientation center that houses a museum and a small auditorium, where a slide show on the mill's history is presented. From the center, trails lead through the 625-acre park to exhibits that include a working reconstructed mill as well as other buildings, nature trails, and scenic overlooks where the Straits and Mackinac Island can be viewed through telescopes. The park is reached from I–75 by departing at exit 338 and heading south on US–23 for 4 miles. Mill Creek (616–436–7301) is open from mid-May to mid-October from 10:00 A.M. to 4:00 P.M. daily. There is an admission fee.

OTSEGO COUNTY

The eastern elk, once a common sight to Indians in the Lower Peninsula, disappeared from Michigan around 1877. After several unsuccessful attempts to re-introduce the animal in the early 1900s, seven Rocky Mountain elk were released in Cheboygan County in 1918, and today biologists believe Michigan's herd of 1,100 elk descended from those animals. The herd ranges over 600 square miles in Cheybogan, Montmorency, Otsego, and Presque Isle counties, but its heaviest concentration is in the wilderness areas of the ❖ **Pigeon River Country State Forest.**

The 95,000-acre state forest features rustic campgrounds, miles of hiking trails, and fishing opportunities, but come fall most visitors have their hearts set on seeing the elk. As big as the adults are (they range from 700 to 900 pounds), they're tough to spot during the summer, for they break up into small groups or are solitary and lie low in the thick forest. But in September the bulls begin the "bugling season," when they move into open areas and form harems of fifteen to twenty cows by calling out to them with a high-pitched whistlelike sound. Elk watchers will see from thirty to a hundred elk gathered in an open field and then hear the most amazing sound—this huge bull making his high-pitched mating call.

To witness one of Michigan's great wildlife scenes, head to the Pigeon River forestry field office, 13 miles east of Vanderbilt, just off Sturgeon River Road. The office is open from 8:00 A.M. to 4:30 P.M. Monday through Friday, and workers can provide maps and suggest open areas to view the elk. The rule of thumb is that two weeks on either side of September 20 is the best time to catch the bugling, or rutting, season. Plan to be at an open area just before dawn or dusk, and sit quietly to await the movement of the herd. One traditional spot to see elk is off Ossmun Road near its junction with Clark Bridge Road northeast of the forestry office. Here you will find a large open field, a small parking lot off the road, and a few elk viewers waiting patiently during September.

CRAWFORD COUNTY

The best-known attraction in this county is ❖ **Hartwick Pines State Park,** where the Virgin Pines Trail loops through a forty-nine-acre stand of virgin white pine and past the Monchard, a 300-year-old pine, one of the most famous trees in the state. Also on the loop is an interpretive center dedicated to Michigan's lumber era at the turn of the century, a reconstructed logger's camp, and various lumber machines on display, including "Big Wheels," used to haul giant logs out of the woods. The state park (517–349–7068) is north of Grayling and can be reached by exiting I–75 at M–93 and following the park signs. The trail is used year-round, but the interpretive center and camp are open only from May through October.

By the time the logging of the late-nineteenth century was finished, much of the state had been reduced to a stump-ridden wasteland. The Civilian Conservation Corps (CCC) replanted the forests, and their story is also told in Crawford County. The ◆ **Civilian Conservation Corps Museum** is located in North Higgins Lake State Park and is dedicated to the program created during President Franklin Roosevelt's administration to help the vast numbers of unemployed men during the Great Depression. It was signed into law as the Emergency Conservation Work Act on March 31, 1933, and by July of that year Michigan had forty-two CCC camps set up that were employing 18,400 men. In all, more than 102,000 Michigan men were enrolled in CCC work projects that involved constructing dams, building hiking trails, stocking lakes, and putting up fire towers. They are best known for planting trees—Michigan during the CCC era led the nation in planting 485 million trees.

The museum is composed of several buildings, including an original cone barn, where workers extracted the seeds from pine cones to be planted later. There is also a replica of a CCC barracks with displays inside that examine the spartan camp life of the men and the duties they performed for $30 a month, of which $22 had to be sent back home to their families. North Higgins Lake State Park (517–821–6125) is reached from US–27 by exiting east on Military Road and from I–75 by heading west at exit 244. There is no admission fee for the CCC museum, but there is a vehicle entry fee for the rest of the park. The museum is open from 10:00 A.M. to 6:00 P.M. from mid-June to Labor Day.

Hunting and fishing has a long tradition in Michigan. How long? In 1994 the state celebrated the one hundredth year in which deer licenses had been issued.

There is no better place to see the history of hunters and anglers in Michigan than at the ◆ **Carl T. Johnson Hunting and Fishing Center,** a state interpretive site in Cadillac. Located adjacent to Mitchell State Park along M–115, the center features a variety of exhibits and hands-on displays, including a marsh diorama, a wall-size aquarium stocked with native fish, and a full-size elk, a species that was re-introduced to the state thanks to the efforts of sportmen's groups. Push a button and you can hear the call of the elk along with the calls of many other Michigan species in the exhibit hall.

From the center a trail leads north into the Heritage Nature Study Area, which includes observation platforms and marshes where you have a reasonably good chance of spotting many of Michigan's wild species.

The Carl T. Johnson Center (616–779–1321) is open Memorial Day through Labor Day from 10:00 A.M. to 8:00 P.M., Tuesday through Sunday. There is a small admission fee.

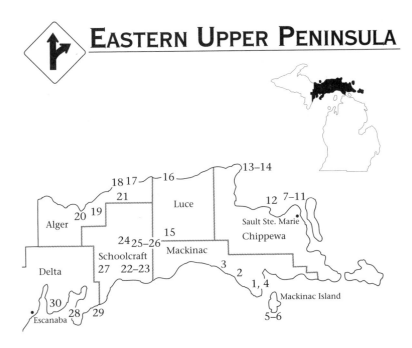

EASTERN UPPER PENINSULA

1. Father Marquette National Memorial
2. Lehto's Pasties
3. Cut River Gorge State Park
4. Marquette Mission Park/ Huron Boardwalk
5. Fort Mackinac
6. Arch Rock
7. SS *Valley Camp*
8. River of History Museum
9. Locks Park Walkway
10. Soo Locks Boat Tours
11. The Antlers
12. Point Iroquois Lightstation
13. Great Lakes Shipwreck Museum
14. Whitefish Point Bird Observatory
15. Helmer House Inn
16. Muskallonge Lake State Park
17. Lefebvre's Fresh & Smoked Fish Market
18. Grand Sable Banks and Dunes
19. Munising Falls
20. Grand Island Venture
21. Au Sable Lightstation
22. Blaney Park
23. Celibeth
24. Seney National Wildlife Refuge
25. Northland Outfitters
26. Eagle's Nest Inn
27. Kitch-Iti-Kipi
28. Fayette State Park
29. Portage Bay State Campground
30. Peninsula Point Lighthouse

EASTERN UPPER PENINSULA

The "Mighty Mac" might sound like a hamburger with the works, but to most Michiganders it's the Mackinac Bridge, the only link between the Lower and Upper peninsulas and the third-longest bridge in the country. Building a bridge was first considered in 1884, but the 5-mile span wasn't built until 1957, finally uniting a state that for its first 120 years was divided by a stretch of water known as the Straits of Mackinac.

Most travelers view the **Mackinac Bridge** as a very scenic drive. A trip across the Mighty Mac is a 360-degree panorama of shorelines, Great Lakes, and islands scattered everywhere, while below the straits bustle with ferries, freighters, and fishing boats. The bridge is also the link between two worlds. Unlike industrialized southern Michigan, the Upper Peninsula's economy was based on lumbering and mining. After the majestic white pines were cut and the mines closed, this section of Michigan fell upon hard times that continue today. Residents of the north, however, are quick to point out that the first permanent settlement in the state was not Detroit but Sault Sainte Marie, that their endurance proves their long history is not about to end anytime soon. Survival is a way of life in the U.P.

What travelers will quickly discover upon crossing the bridge is a place of remote beauty and unique character, where interstate highways are almost nonexistent, and motel chains and fast-food restaurants are few and far between. Almost every road in the U.P. is "off the beaten path," offering natural beauty, family-run inns and cafes, and outdoor opportunities that will satisfy any lover of pristine forests, lakes, and streams.

MACKINAC COUNTY

The view from Mighty Mac is excellent, but the best view of the bridge itself is from the north shore at ❖ **Father Marquette National Memorial,** just outside St. Ignace. Father Marquette, a newly ordained Jesuit priest from France, paddled his way through the Great Lakes and founded Sault Sainte Marie in 1668, founded St. Ignace three years later, and then joined Louis Jolliet on a 3,000-mile paddle discovering the Mississippi

River. He did this—along with converting thousands of Indians to Christianity—in only nine years, dying on the banks of Lake Michigan in 1675.

To celebrate the tricentennial of Marquette's discovery of the Mississippi, a presidential committee chose St. Ignace as the site of a permanent memorial. Also on the grounds is a museum (open 8:00 A.M. to 8:00 P.M. daily June 1 through Labor Day) that includes displays on Marquette and the Indian tribes he encountered, an auditorium with a sixteen-minute film on the life of the priest, and perhaps most intriguing, a replica of the explorer's Mississippi journal in both the original French and an English translation. Here you can flip through the pages and read segments of this man's incredible odyssey.

Outside the museum there is an overlook with a public telescope that gives you a sweeping view of the Mackinac Bridge. There are posted exits to the park from both I–75 and US–2.

A portion of US–2 west of St. Ignace is gradually becoming a row of motels, convenience stores, and cafes—one business little different from the next, but one notable establishment is worth a stop. Some 8 miles west of town is ◆ **Lehto's Pasties,** the first of many pasties shops you are bound to see in the U.P. The Cornish pasty, an Upper Peninsula specialty, looks like a king-size apple turnover crust, but it is filled with meat, potatoes, onion, and a little rutabaga for flavor. Pasties were supper for the miners, who could take the pies down the shafts and at mealtime heat them on their shovels with the candles on their helmets. Although many believe they originated in the U.P. copper mines in the mid-1800s, they actually date back much earlier, to mining days in Cornwall, England.

The lunch counter run by John and Katherine Lehto doesn't look like much, but they have been making pasties since 1947, when John arrived at St. Ignace to take a job on the Straits of Mackinac ferry and his wife opened up the "pasty drive-in." Business was so good that John quit his state job three years later and built the small eatery. Nothing has changed since then—certainly not their pasties, which are hard to beat anywhere in the north. Pasties to go are $3.50 each, and it's an extra dollar if you want to occupy one of the eight seats at the lunch counter. Lehto's Pasties is open May through November from 8:30 A.M. until 6:00 P.M. or whenever they run out of pasties.

Scenic shoreline drives abound in Michigan, but it's hard to argue when someone claims the most spectacular of them all is the stretch of US–2 from St. Ignace to the Hamlet of Naubinway. The views of Lake Michigan, beaches, dunes, and offshore island are rarely interrupted along this 42-mile segment. One of the places to spot for a panoramic view on this drive is ◈ **Cut River Gorge Roadside Park** on US–2, 26 miles west of St. Ignace.

Actually there are three parks on both sides of this stunning gorge that are connected by the impressive Cut River Bridge, a steel arch cantilever structure that was built in 1948 and stands 147 feet above the river. You can walk across the bridge for an impressive view of Lake Michigan or follow one of three foot trails that wind down to the Cut River and then out to a beautiful beach on the Great Lake. By combining the two trails with a walk across the bridge itself, you'll enjoy an interesting loop of between 1 and 1.3 miles.

A much less traveled but equally scenic route is east of the Mackinac Bridge on M–134. The road follows the U.P. shoreline along northern Lake Huron, passing the intriguing Les Cheneaux Islands and ending at De Tour, the departure point for remote Drummond Island, a haven of fishing resorts. The best stretch is the 24 miles from Cedarville in Mackinac County to De Tour in Chippewa County. This segment is one continuous view of the lake, the islands, and long stretches of sand where there are more than a dozen turnoffs and roadside parks, allowing everybody an uncrowded beach for a lazy afternoon in the sun.

Sometimes in our rush to see one place, we overlook another. Such is often the case of a place like St. Ignace. This historical town, the second oldest settlement in Michigan, has a scenic harbor and a main street full of shops and restaurants. Only who takes the time to look around when we're all racing through in an effort to catch the next boat to Mackinac Island?

Slow down. St. Ignace is an intriguing city, and you don't have to go any farther than ◈ **Marquette Mission Park and Huron Boardwalk** to discover why. The recently completed boardwalk winds 2 miles from near the historical park, and together they take you back more than 300 years into the life of this town.

Marquette Mission Park features Father Marquette's grave and several outdoor exhibits that retrace the significance of this little plot of land. From the park you then cross the street to Huron Boardwalk, which winds south along the St. Ignace waterfront. The boardwalk features its own series of historical displays, which cover everything from "Nineteenth-Century St. Ignace" to the "Legacy of White Pine" in text and photos. In between the displays are benches, each with a million-dollar view of Mackinac Island, the ferries making high-speed runs to the resort island, and the rest of the bustling waterfront.

To reach Marquette Mission Park and Huron Boardwalk from I–75 on the north side of the Mackinac Bridge, take exit 344A and follow Business Loop I–75 to State Street, which parallels the boardwalk.

There are numerous forts to visit in Michigan, but without a doubt the most famous and probably the most beloved is ◆ **Fort Mackinac** on Mackinac Island. Built and first occupied by the British in 1779, the fort is part of Mackinac Island State Park and is the scene of cannon firings and other living-history demonstrations throughout the summer. The **Officer's Stone Quarters,** constructed of limestone in 1781, is the oldest known building still standing in Michigan. The scene of the white stockade looming above the island's downtown area is probably one of the most photographed in the state.

The fort is open daily during the summer and is one of several museums within the downtown area of Mackinac Island. There is a single admission fee to all the museums.

Mackinac Island State Park actually covers 1,800 acres, or 83 percent of the island, and offers much more than just cannon demonstrations twice a day. There are 140 miles of roads and trails, open to use by hikers, cyclists, and equestrians but not cars, as they are not allowed on the island. The roads and trails loop through a surprisingly rugged and wooded terrain, past some of the most interesting natural formations in Michigan, including ◆ **Arch Rock,** the almost perfect 50-foot-wide limestone arch. The vast majority of visitors reach these attractions on a bicycle, which can either be brought to the island on the ferries or rented in the downtown area.

For more information on the Mackinac Island State Park, call (906) 847–3328, beginning in mid-May. For information on the three ferry companies that provide transport to the island, call St. Ignace Chamber of Commerce at (800) 338–6660.

129

CHIPPEWA COUNTY

Sault Sainte Marie is synonymous with the Soo Locks, the world's largest and busiest locking system, the crucial link for freighters passing from Lake Superior to Lake Huron. The city of 15,000 is Michigan's oldest and has been an important center since the French Canadian voyagers in the 1700s portaged their long canoes and bales of furs around St. Mary's Rapids.

Most of this colorful history of shipping can be appreciated by walking along Water Street, beginning at its east end, where the ◆ SS *Valley Camp* is docked next to the Chamber of Commerce Information Center. The 550-foot freighter was once owned and used by Republic Steel Corporation and frequently passed through the locks. Today it has been turned into one of the largest Great Lakes marine museums and is listed as a national historic site. From the pilothouse and the 1800-horsepower steam engine to the captain's quarters and the galley, visitors are free to roam the ship for a close-up look at life aboard an ore carrier, where a crew of almost thirty worked, slept, and ate. Down below, in its massive cargo holds, are models and displays of Great Lake vessels, aquariums of the freshwater fish that abound nearby, and a room devoted to wreckage of the *Edmund Fitzgerald,* the ore carrier that sank in the raging Lake Superior in 1975, taking its captain and crew of twenty-eight with it.

The SS *Valley Camp* (906–632–3658) is open daily from 10:00 A.M. to 6:00 P.M. May 15 to June 30; 9:00 A.M. to 9:00 P.M. July 1 to August 31; and 10:00 A.M. to 6:00 P.M. September 1 to October 16. There is an admission fee.

The newest stop in any tour of the city is the ◆ **River of History Museum,** which opened in 1993. Through the use of eight exhibit galleries and a state-of-the-art audio system, the museum takes you on an 8,000-year journey along the shores of St. Mary's River. You begin with the sounds of ice melting and the rapids roaring as a glacier carves out the river valley. You move onto the sprawling Indian camp that was once here and then see the first French explorers paddling ashore in 1662.

The River of History Museum (906–632–1999) is at 209 East Portage Avenue. It's open May 15 to October 15 from 10:00 A.M. to 5:00 P.M. Monday through Saturday and noon to 5:00 P.M. Sunday.

To reach the locks to the north, return to and follow Water Street, which in 1982 was renovated into the ◆**Locks Park Walkway,** providing an excellent overview of the city's 350-year past. The walkway is marked by blue symbols of freighters, and interpretive plaques explain the history of various areas and renovated buildings. Along the way you'll pass the Baraga House, the 1864 home of missionary and historian Bishop Frederic Baraga, the "Snowshoe Saint" and first bishop of the U.P. Nearby is the Johnston House, which was constructed in 1794 for an Irish fur trader, making it the oldest surviving home in Michigan. The walkway also passes the site of Fort Brady, built by the Americans in 1823, and the spot where in 1820 General Lewis Cass lowered and removed the last British flag to fly over U.S. soil.

Water Street ends at Soo Lock Park in the heart of downtown Sault Sainte Marie. The U.S. Army Corps of Engineers maintains the park and visitor's center, and next to the locks they built a raised viewing platform that provides an excellent view of ships being raised and lowered to the different lake levels. You can experience the locks directly through ◆**Soo Locks Boat Tours.** For an admission fee, people take a two-hour cruise up and down St. Mary's River, first passing through an American lock and then returning through the Canadian one. Boats depart daily from May 15 through October 15, beginning at 9:00 A.M. and ending with the last cruise at 5:30 P.M. Soo Locks Boat Tours (906–632–2512) maintains two docks, both on Portage Avenue south of the SS *Valley Camp.*

As well known to locals as the locks is ◆**The Antlers,** an Irish bar and restaurant on Portage Avenue. The exterior of the simple stone building that houses the seventy-five-year-old eatery is misleading. Inside, the decor is a museum of collectibles (or some say junk), including hundreds of mounted animals on the walls, a birch-bark canoe hanging from the ceiling, and a 15-foot boa constrictor overlooking the bar. No wall is left bare. Hockey great Gordie Howe (whose picture also adorns the walls) was a frequent patron of the restaurant, which is known for its steaks and "Paul Bunyan" hamburgers. The Antlers (906–632–3571) is open daily from 11:00 A.M. to 10:00 P.M., and dinner prices range from $6.00 to $15.00.

One of the more interesting drives in the U.P. follows Whitefish Bay, beginning at Brimley (reached from M–28) and ending at desolate Whitefish Point. At Brimley follow Lake Shore Drive to the west as it hugs the shoreline, with frequent views of beaches and Lake Superior. In 7.5 miles, you'll come to ✦ **Point Iroquois Lightstation.** The classic lighthouse was built in 1870 and operated until 1963, when sophisticated radar made it obsolete. The Coast Guard turned it over to the U.S. Forestry Service, which worked with local historical societies to open it to the public in 1984. It has since been added to the National Register of Historic Places and features a few displays and artifacts in three rooms of the lightkeeper's house. This lighthouse is mainly popular for its climbing curved staircase of seventy steps that leads to the top of the tower and a view of the surrounding area. The panorama, needless to say, is impressive, as you can see almost the entire coastline of Whitefish Bay and miles out into Lake Superior, including any freighter that happens to be passing by. The lightstation is open Memorial Day through Labor Day 9:00 A.M. to 7:00 P.M. daily.

Lake Shore Drive, with its numerous pulloffs and scenic beaches, ends when it merges into M–123. The state road is well traveled, as it first heads north along the shoreline of Whitefish Bay and then at Paradise swings west to head inland to Tahquamenon Falls. Though the popular falls, the second-largest east of the Mississippi River (Niagara Falls is the largest), is the destination for most travelers, there is a good reason to continue heading north on Whitefish Point Road. At the very end of the road, at the very tip of the remote peninsula that juts out into Lake Superior, is the ✦ **Great Lakes Shipwreck Museum.** Whitefish Point is a combination of sandy beach, small dunes, and thunderous Lake Superior waves crashing along the shoreline. It also marks the east end of an 80-mile stretch that sailors knew as the "Graveyard of the Great Lakes." Raging northwest storms, built up over 200 miles of open water, have caused 300 recorded shipwrecks in which 320 seamen have died along this section of shoreline.

The Great Lakes Shipwreck Historical Society, a group of divers researching the wrecks, opened the museum in 1986 in abandoned buildings of the Coast Guard Station, whose light, beaming since 1849, is the oldest active one on Lake Superior. In the main museum, each display is devoted to a different shipwreck. Visitors see a drawing or photograph of the vessel and

Point Iroquois Lightstation

artifacts that divers have collected, and read the story of its fatal voyage. The ships range from sailing schooners of the early 1800s to the *Edmund Fitzgerald,* the latest and largest shipwreck, which continues to fascinate residents of the U.P. A darkened interior with theatrical lights, soft music, and special sound effects of sea gulls and fog horns sends tingles down the spines of most people.

Another building has been turned into a theater where underwater films of the wrecks are shown, and eventually the lightkeeper's house will be open to visitors. The museum is open from Memorial Day until mid-October daily from 10:00 A.M. to 6:00 P.M. There is an admission fee.

Most of the point is a state wildlife sanctuary, renowned for the variety of birds that pass through. The Michigan

Audubon Society has established the ❖**Whitefish Point Bird Observatory,** across from the lightstation, where a small information room tells birders the species to be watching for as they hike along the point's network of trails.

LUCE COUNTY

The county that lies between Chippewa and Alger is probably best known for the Two Hearted River, fished by Ernest Hemingway and later the setting for one of his stories. Today it remains a favorite for anglers and canoers, who enjoy the solitude of this remote wilderness river that empties into Lake Superior.

For travelers in Luce County who want to spend their nights in comfort at an inn or hotel, there are two interesting places, well worth the out-of-the-way drive to reach them. One is the ❖**Helmer House Inn,** located on the northeast corner of Manistique Lake near the Luce-Mackinac county line. To reach it, you head north from US–2 on County Road H–33 and then swing onto County Road 417. The inn was built in 1881 by a minister as a mission for early settlers; Gale Helmer turned it into a general store and resort six years later. The area thrived as a summer getaway, so the federal government set up a post office in the inn, appointed Helmer postmaster, and named the spot, for lack of a better name, Helmer.

The post office lasted only nineteen years, and eventually the building was abandoned. Rob Goldthorpe and his wife renovated the lodge and reopened it in 1982. Today the inn is a state historic site and offers five guest rooms, all furnished with antiques. The lodge is probably better known, however, for its wraparound porch that was glassed in and turned into a delightful little restaurant. Every table has a view of the rural setting outside, and the menu includes steaks, fish, and, occasionally, stuffed trout. The small salad bar is excellent.

Overnight guests are treated to a full breakfast in the morning as well as a soft bed at night. Rooms, which have shared bathrooms, range from $36 to $55 for singles or doubles. The restaurant is open 3:00 to 9:00 P.M. daily from May to mid-October and noon to 9:00 P.M. daily in July and August. For room reservations write to the Helmer House Inn at McMillan 49853, or call (906–586–3204).

The other pleasant spot in Luce County to spend a night is ◆ **Muskallonge Lake State Park** at the north end of County Road H–37 in the northwest corner of the county. The park is actually a strip of land lying between Muskallonge Lake, known for its pike, perch, and smallmouth bass fishing, and Lake Superior. You can camp on a site overlooking the small lake and then wander over to Lake Superior to enjoy its seemingly endless sandy shoreline. There is a vehicle fee to enter Muskallonge Lake State Park (906–658–3338) and an overnight fee of $13 for one of its 179 campsites.

ALGER COUNTY

Pasties are the best-known dish U.P. cooks serve, but another delicacy of the north is smoked fish. Driving the shoreline roads along Lake Superior, you'll see a number of smokehouses offering whitefish, lake trout, herring, and menominee, but no one does it better than Vern Kirkens of Grand Marais. Kirkens has been smoking fish since the early 1960s and today runs ◆ **Lefebvre's Fresh & Smoked Fish Market** located in town off H–58. Kirkens says the best fish is smoked with hardwood (he uses sugar maple), but that some houses try to cut costs by using mostly propane. If you have never eaten smoked fish, first try lake trout, which has a much more delicate flavor than whitefish or herring. Break off large chunks and enjoy them with a bit of sharp cheddar cheese on a slice of dark bread while sipping an ice-cold beer on the sandy shoreline of Grand Marais. Many think it's the Upper Peninsula at its finest.

The Lefebvre Fresh & Smoked Fish Market (906–494–2563) is open from 8:00 A.M. to 6:00 P.M. Wednesday through Monday daily from mid-May until early December. The shop also sells smoked turkey, homemade beef jerky, and pies, turnovers, and sticky cinnamon buns that Kirkens's wife bakes daily.

Grand Marais, a booming lumbertown of 2,500 at the turn of the century, is a sleepy hamlet of 400 today and the gateway for the eastern half of Pictured Rocks National Lakeshore. The National Park Service maintains the **Grand Marais Ranger Station and Maritime Museum** (906–494–2669) near the harbor. It provides maps and information on the park along with a sailor's history of the area. One spot they will undoubtedly urge you to see within the park is the ◆ **Grand Sable Banks and Dunes.**

To reach the sandy hills, follow County Road H–58 west of town, first passing the parking lot and short side trail to Sable Falls and then the Grand Sable Visitor Center. From both places there are half-mile trails that lead to the Grand Sable Dunes. Or you can continue following the county road a mile past the visitor's center until the pavement ends. On one side of the road is the picnic area and beach of Grand Sable Lake, and on the other side is a huge dune. There are no more than 50 yards between the lake and this mountain of sand. Visitors first tackle the heartpounding scramble up the dune, where at the top there's a magnificent view of the windswept sand, Grand Sable Lake, and Lake Superior off in the distance. Then it's a mad dash down the steep bank of sand and usually right into the lake to cool off.

The dunes are a 4-square-mile area of sandy hills about half as high as Sleeping Bear Dunes in the Lower Peninsula, but no less impressive. They end with the Grand Sable Banks, steep sandy bluffs some 300 feet tall that tower right above the Lake Superior shoreline. The best view is obtained by turning off H–58 onto a marked side road for the **log slide** located 8 miles west of Grand Marais. A short boardwalk leads to a breathtaking overlook 300 feet above Lake Superior, where to the west Au Sable Point Lighthouse is silhouetted against the water and to the east the banks curve 5 miles back toward Grand Marais. Down below is the 500-foot wooden slide that loggers used in the 1800s to send trees into Lake Superior on their way to town. The lighthouse, which was built in 1874, has been renovated by the National Park Service and is an easy 1.5-mile hike from Hurricane River Campground located farther west on H–58.

You could continue along H–58, although only about half of it is paved, and end up in Munising. The scenic town is the gateway to the **Pictured Rocks,** sandstone cliffs that rise 50 to 200 feet above Lake Superior and stretch for 15 miles to the west. They are one of the top attractions in the U.P., and during the summer visitors take a Pictured Rock cruise or drive to its most famous formation, Miner's Castle.

Equally as impressive as Miner's Castle and much closer to town is ◆ **Munising Falls.** From H–58 head up Sand Point Road a short way to the National Park Visitor Center, where a quarter-mile path takes you into the woods and up a shaded sandstone canyon. The first viewing platform provides a fine overview of the 50-foot cascade that tumbles straight down a sandstone cliff; a nearby stairway allows you to walk up to the falls for a most unusual view of the falling water.

Munising is also on the edge of another park, the Alger Underwater Preserve, a graveyard of shipwrecks that date back to the 1800s and early 1900s. The preserve and especially the waters around Grand Island are a haven for scuba divers who view the wrecks that lie 10 to 100 feet below the surface. But nondivers can also enjoy the treasures of Lake Superior with ◈ **Grand Island Venture,** a charter service out of Munising. Captain Peter Lindquist takes snorkelers into the preserve, where they can view a number of wrecks, including the *Dreadnaught,* a three-mast schooner that lies off Grand Island only 10 feet below the surface. The ship, which dates back to the 1880s, is still intact with a complete hull. Other wrecks lie 20 to 30 feet below the surface, but in Lake Superior's crystal-clear water, even snorkelers can get a good view of them.

The cost is $20 per person for each wreck; a two-wreck trip lasts two and a half hours. Often wet suits are not necessary for the swims, but if additional warmth is needed, the suits can be rented next door at Sea & Ski Scuba (906–387–2927). You can write to Grand Island Travel Service at Mill Street, Route 1, P.O. Box 436, Munising 49862, or call (906–387–4477).

Want to see shipwrecks without swimming in frigid Lake Superior? Then return to Pictured Rocks National Lakeshore and head up County Road H–58 to Hurricane River Campground. East of the campground Lakeshore Trail becomes an old access road to ◈ **Au Sable Lightstation,** and near its trailhead is a SHIPWRECKS sign pointing down to the beach. These ruins lie in the water and are hard to spot when there is a chop on the lake. Walk another mile and a half up the trail, and you'll see a second shipwreck sign that directs you to three sets of ruins half buried in the sandy beach.

SCHOOLCRAFT COUNTY

◈ **Blaney Park** is the town that refuses to die. It's been foreclosed on, boarded up, even auctioned off building by building, but today the village is surging back as a quiet resort with an ideal location for touring the Upper Peninsula. No more than ninety minutes from this one-road hamlet are the U.P.'s most popular attractions: Tahquamenon Falls, Pictured Rocks, the historic townsite of Fayette, and miles of Lake Michigan's sandy shoreline.

Originally a logging camp, Blaney and the area around it were logged out by 1926, so its owners searched for another endeavor for the town's residents. With all the lakes and sandy beach nearby, recreation was the answer, and soon Blaney became Blaney Park. Tourists began arriving from all over the Midwest to spend their vacations on the Upper Peninsula. The resort featured a nine-hole golf course, tennis courts, riding stables, daily excursions to Lake Michigan beaches, and a lighted swimming pool for those who preferred to stay close to their cottages. A lumber baron's mansion was renamed Celibeth and was described in one brochure as "a beautiful club-type hotel." The boardinghouse where loggers had lived was turned into a twenty-one-room lodge, and, in 1934, Blaney Inn was built, a huge dining facility that featured stone fireplaces, walls paneled in knotty pine, and seating for 400.

Improved roads in the Upper Peninsula were Blaney Park's downfall. The family that owned the town tried twice to sell it, only to inherit it again when the buyers defaulted on the payments. The last tourist season was in 1972, after which many of the buildings were boarded up, and Blaney Park finally was auctioned off in 1985. Celibeth was purchased by Elisa Strom, who once worked as a waitress at the resort. After spending more than a year restoring the mansion, she reopened it in 1987 as a bed and breakfast.

The twenty-two-room ◆**Celibeth** has nine bedrooms decorated with antiques and furnishings from the Blaney Park resort period. There is an enclosed porch that overlooks the front lawn and features a row of rocking chairs and a 1913 hand-cranked phonograph, a reading room stocked with issues of *Life* magazines from the 1950s, and a sunroom where a leisurely breakfast is served. Down the street the lodge is still boarded up, but the rest of the resort town is slowly coming alive. You can once again enjoy dinner at the Blaney Inn, browse through a woodcarving-gift shop, or stop at the old school, now a grocery store whose front walls are covered with fading photographs of Blaney Park in the 1940s.

From the Mackinac Bridge follow US–2 west for 66 miles and then turn north on M–77 for a mile to reach the town. The bed and breakfast (906–283–3409) is open year-round, and the rooms range from $40 to $50 per night.

The heart of Schoolcraft County, some 96,000 acres, has been preserved as the largest wildlife refuge east of the Mississippi River. The ◆ **Seney National Wildlife Refuge** was established in 1935 by the U.S. Fish and Wildlife Service to provide a habitat for wildlife, primarily waterfowl migrating to nesting grounds in Canada. The refuge surrounds the Great Manistique Swamp, which endured rough treatment beginning in the 1870s, when loggers were intent on stripping every tree from the area. Fires were then deliberately set to clear away the debris of the lumbering operation, preventing new forests from taking root. Finally a land development company came through, drained acre after acre of the swamp, and sold the land to farmers for agriculture in 1911. The farmers lasted about a year, discovering they had been swindled—the soil would grow little.

Seney was a wasteland that nobody wanted. The state ended up with it and during the Great Depression deeded it to the federal government with the recommendation that it be turned into a refuge. Civilian Conservation Corps workers came in and built dikes, dug ditches, and used other water-control devices to impound 7,000 acres of water in twenty-one major ponds, almost miraculously restoring the marsh. Seney again became a habitat for waterfowl when 332 Canada geese were released in 1936 and established its present nesting flocks. Still more geese and other species of birds depend on the area as an important rest stop on their long migration to nesting sites in Canada.

Other wildlife—timber wolves, deer, black bears, moose, and coyotes—live in the refuge, but the Canada goose has clearly become the symbol of Seney's return to wilderness. You will see the "honkers" the minute you drive into the parking lot of the visitor's center, as a few tame ones are always around looking for a handout from soft-hearted tourists. The center overlooks one of the many ponds in the refuge, and a telescope at its large viewing window lets you search the marsh area for some of the more than 200 species of birds that can be found there. The center has displays, a children's touch table, and an auditorium that hosts nature movies and slide programs each hour. It is open from May

15 through September 30 from 9:00 A.M. until 5:00 P.M. daily.

The best way to view the wildlife is to follow the 7-mile **Marshland Wildlife Drive** in your car as it winds its way among the ponds, starting near the center and ending at M–77 just south of the refuge entrance. Pick up a free guide that points out items of interest at a number of marked stops, including an active bald eagle nest that can be seen clearly from the drive. Timing is important for spotting wildlife, and it is best to follow the drive either in early morning or at dusk when the animals are most active. Often during the peak of the tourist season, the refuge will stage guided evening tours that depart around 6:00 P.M. and last for almost two hours. Call the visitor's center (906–586–9851) for information regarding the auto tours.

Another unique way to view more remote areas of the refuge is to paddle the handful of rivers that flow through it. ❖ **Northland Outfitters** (906–586–9801) is located in nearby Germfask and offers canoe rentals for the area. The outfitters will supply canoes, paddles, life jackets, and transportation to the Manistique River, which runs through the southeast corner of Seney. The trips are self-guided, last either two or four hours, and offer the possibilities of spotting beavers, deer, otters, and a variety of birds or of fishing for walleye or pike in the river. Next to the outfitters is ❖ **Eagle's Nest Inn,** a restaurant housed in one of the original refuge buildings constructed in the late 1930s. The inn now looks like a Cape Cod–style eatery and specializes in whitefish, perch, and lake trout from the Great Lakes. Hours are 11:30 A.M. until 8:00 P.M. daily except Monday from mid-April through November. Dinners range from $10 to $16.

On the opposite scale of parks is Palms Brook, a state park of only 388 acres located 12 miles northwest of Manistique on M–149. The park may be small, but it's equally intriguing due to ❖ **Kitch-Iti-Kipi,** Michigan's largest spring. The natural spring pours out more than 10,000 gallons of water per minute from fissures in the underlying limestone and has created a crystal-clear pool 200 feet wide and 40 feet deep. Visitors board a wooden raft with observation holes in the middle and pull themselves across the spring to get a good view of the fantasy world below. Between the swirls of sand and ghostly bubbles rising up, you can view ancient trees with branches encrusted in limestone, huge brown trout slipping silently by, and colors and shapes that challenge the imagination. The spring is especially enchanting in the early morning, when a mist lies over the water and the trout rise to the surface. Palms Brook has a picnic area but no campsites, and there is a vehicle fee to enter. The raft is free.

DELTA COUNTY

In the mid-1800s, iron ore was shipped from the Upper Peninsula mines to the foundries in the lower Great Lakes at a tremendous cost to companies. The high price of shipping was due to the inefficient method of transportation coupled with the nearly 40 percent waste the ore contained. Fayette Brown, general manager of the Jackson Iron Company, studied the problem and decided the solution was to build a company-owned furnace not far from the mine, where the ore could be smelted into pig iron before it was shipped to the steel-making centers. The town he planned to build had to be a reasonable distance from the Escanaba ore docks, possess a natural harbor, and be near large amounts of limestone and hardwood forests that were needed to smelt the iron ore. In 1866 Brown chose a spot on Garden Peninsula overlooking Big Bay de Noc, and the town of Fayette was born.

A year later the work began on the furnace and charcoal kiln, and by Christmas the first iron from Fayette was cast. Quickly a town emerged. There was the superintendent's house on a bluff overlooking the harbor, a company office, nine frame dwellings for the engineers and skilled workers, and forty log cabins for the unskilled laborers. Eventually Fayette featured a machine shop, small railroad, barns, blacksmith shop, hotel, and even an opera house. It was a total community that in 1884 had a population of almost 1,000 and turned out 16,875 tons of iron. Toward the end of that decade, however, Fayette's fate was sealed. The price of pig iron fell, and newly developed coke blast furnaces produced a higher quality iron at a much cheaper rate. In 1891 the company closed down the furnaces, and within a few years Fayette became a ghost town.

Fayette changed hands several times; at last the state of Michigan obtained the area in 1959 and turned it into ◆ **Fayette State Park.** The town booms again as a scenic ghost town overlooking Snail Shell Harbor, with its towering white cliffs. The 365-acre park is reached from US–2 on County Road

Charcoal Kiln in Fayette State Park

483 and contains an interpretive museum with information, guide maps, and a scale model of Fayette during its heyday. From there you leisurely wander among twenty-two existing buildings, of which nine are open. The renovated structures, which are furnished, include the company office, the hotel, the opera house, and a home of one of the skilled employees. More will be opened up in the future.

Fayette State Park (906–644–2603) also has eighty campsites, a beach and picnic area, and boat-launching facilities. The museum is open daily May 15 to October 15 from 9:00 A.M. to 5:00 P.M. and until 6:00 P.M. from Memorial Day to Labor Day. There is a vehicle fee to enter the park and an $8.00-per-night fee to camp.

Another spot worth searching out on Garden Peninsula is

❖ **Portage Bay State Campground,** which is reached from County Road 483 (before the state park) by turning off on County Road 08 and carefully following the signs. The rustic campground (no electricity, pit toilets) is a bumpy 5-mile ride along dirt roads, but the camping area is worth it: You pitch your tent or park your trailer among the pine trees that border the sandy beach of the bay. You can stroll along the beach; follow the hiking trails in the area, or take a dip in the clear water of Lake Michigan.

A delightful picnic area in Delta County is ❖ **Peninsula Point Lighthouse,** the guiding light at the very tip of Stonington Peninsula that was built in 1865. Congress authorized the funds the year before, because the wooden sailing ships hauling lumber, iron ore, and fish from Escanaba and Fayette were no match for the treacherous shoals and reefs that separated Big Bay de Noc from Little Bay de Noc. The light went out for the last time in 1936, and the house portion of the lighthouse burned to the ground in 1959. But the view from the point was so spectacular that the Forest Service made it into a public picnic area in 1937.

Climb the forty steps to the top of the square brick tower, and you're greeted with a 360-degree panorama that includes the Escanaba waterfront to the west, the limestone bluffs of Fayette State Park to the east, and the length of Lake Michigan in front of you. You can either hike to it or drive in. The 1.5-mile hike is a scenic walk, while the final mile to the nineteenth-century light is a narrow, winding, and very bumpy one-lane road not recommended for recreational vehicles more than 16 feet long or 8 feet high.

To reach the lighthouse from Rapid River, head east on US–2 to the Stonington exit. Head south 19 miles on County Road 513 to Stonington, and then take Forest Road 2204. The RV parking area and trailhead are reached before the forest road turns into a narrow, one-lane road in the final mile.

WESTERN UPPER PENINSULA

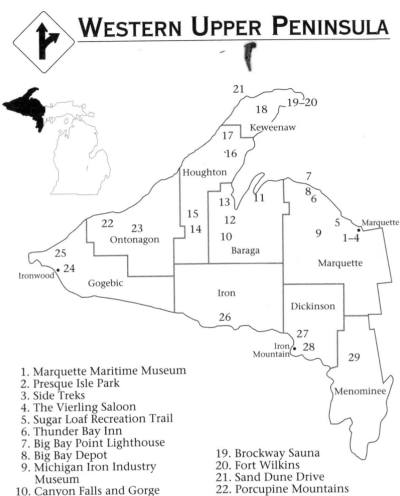

21
18
19–20
Keweenaw
17
16
Houghton
13
11
7
8
6
15
12
5
Marquette
22
23
14
10
9
1–4
Ontonagon
Baraga
25
24
Marquette
Ironwood
Gogebic
Iron
Dickinson
26
27
Iron 28
Mountain
29
Menominee

1. Marquette Maritime Museum
2. Presque Isle Park
3. Side Treks
4. The Vierling Saloon
5. Sugar Loaf Recreation Trail
6. Thunder Bay Inn
7. Big Bay Point Lighthouse
8. Big Bay Depot
9. Michigan Iron Industry
   Museum
10. Canyon Falls and Gorge
11. Mount Arvon
12. Hilltop Restaurant
13. Hanka Homestead
14. Sturgeon River Gorge Area
15. Silver Mountain
16. Lindell's Chocolate Shop
17. Calumet Opera House
18. Delaware Mine

19. Brockway Sauna
20. Fort Wilkins
21. Sand Dune Drive
22. Porcupine Mountains
    Wilderness State Park
23. Old Victoria
24. Black River Harbor Drive
25. Bear Track Inn
26. Iron County Museum
27. The Stables
28. Piers Gorge
29. IXL Office Museum

WESTERN UPPER PENINSULA

Michigan's most remote and rustic region is the rugged western Upper Peninsula. Two small ranges located here constitute the only true mountains in any of the Great Lakes states; between Baraga and Marquette lie the Huron Mountains, and along the Lake Superior shoreline, from west of Ontonagon to Copper Harbor, is the Copper Range. Within these rugged hills are Mount Arvon, the highest point in Michigan at 1,979 feet above sea level, and the Porcupine Mountains, between whose ridges and peaks lies the stunning Lake of the Clouds.

It was in these hills of the western U.P. that the great iron and copper mines flourished from the 1800s to the 1940s, bringing boatloads of immigrants from Norway, Finland, and Italy to work in the shafts. Today the remnants of the mining era are ghost towns, abandoned mines, and communities with strong ethnic heritage and pride.

For most Michigan residents, this region of the state is a remote, distant place; driving to Copper Harbor from Detroit is the same distance as traveling to Washington, D.C. But once it is "discovered," travelers marvel at the western U.P.'s natural wonders. More than for its mines, pasty shops, and historical museums, you come to this region of Michigan for the beauty of nature's handiwork: cascading waterfalls, panoramas of forested wilderness, a lake set in a sea of reds, yellows, and oranges painted by autumn leaves.

MARQUETTE COUNTY

The largest county in Michigan includes 1,873 square miles, 1,800 lakes, 73 miles of Lake Superior shoreline, and Marquette, the largest (and some say, only) city in the Upper Peninsula. The city of 23,000 became a spot on the map with a post office in 1849, and it bloomed the following decade as the port and shipping center for the nearby iron mines and logging camps. The lumber and mining barons graced the streets of Marquette with mansions, many still standing today. From Front Street turn east onto Ridge Street and you'll head toward Lake Superior, passing one late-Victorian home after another until you end up in the parking lot of the ◆**Marquette Maritime Museum** on the waterfront.

The museum is housed in the red sandstone Old Water Works Building and features displays on shipwrecks, antique outboard motors and boats, commercial fishermen who worked the area, and other facets of the city's maritime days, which fed many and made some (from the look of their homes) incredibly wealthy. Open from Memorial Day until mid-September, the museum can be viewed from 10:00 A.M. until 5:00 P.M. daily. A small admission fee is charged.

The largest and most interesting structures on Marquette's waterfront are the iron ore docks that load the Great Lakes freighters with the rock for a journey south. There are two interesting places in town to view them. The Lake Superior and Ishpeming Railroad docks are still operating today, and the best vantage point is ◆ **Presque Isle Park.** The 328-acre city park is not an isle but a peninsula that juts out into Lake Superior on the north side of Marquette. A road circles the park shoreline, beginning on the south side, where you can see the ore docks and, if your timing is right, watch a freighter receive its load (one to three times a week).

The drive continues and passes the steep red cliffs of Lookout Point and then the view at Sunset Point, where residents gather to watch the end of another day. The park also has an outdoor band shell with weekly events, a small zoo, a beach and bathhouse, picnic areas, and bicycle paths. Hiking trails crisscross the forested interior of Presque Isle and become a favorite spot for Nordic skiers during the winter. The park is open daily from 7:00 A.M. until 11:00 P.M., and perhaps the best time of year to visit it is the last weekend in July during its Art-on-the-Rocks Festival, when local artists gather to display and sell their work in this picturesque setting.

A unique way to view Presque Isle is from the seat of a sea-touring kayak during sunset or in the moonlight. ◆ **Side Treks** offers tours throughout the summer as well as other guided trips to Pictured Rocks National Lakeshore, Grand Island, and the rugged coastline just north of Marquette.

All trips include a kayak, paddling equipment, instruction, and transportation. The cost of day trips ranges from $39 to $79. Bookings can be made by calling Side Treks at (906) 228–8735 or by stopping in at Down Wind Sports, 514 N. Street in Marquette.

In Marquette's Lower Harbor are the Old Ore Docks, no longer operating, which have been designated a state historic site. An

147

excellent place to view the docks is from a table in ◆ **The Vierling Saloon** on the corner of Front and Main streets. The saloon was opened in 1883 by Martin Vierling, an art lover and saloon keeper who headed north with his paintings after running an establishment in Detroit. Later the art lover's bar became just another cafe during prohibition, but the present proprietors, Terry and Christi Doyle, have turned back the clock by renovating the interior and returning the building to its original function as a saloon and fine restaurant. The brick walls inside once again feature paintings and prints, as the owners exhibit the works of a different artist every month. There are also old photographs and artifacts of early Marquette, and the large windows in the rear of the restaurant overlook the iron ore docks. A pair of binoculars hangs on the back wall for anyone wanting a closer look at the massive structure.

The fare is "geared to healthy food," and the dinner menu features several shrimp and chicken entrees and Rogan Josh, an Indian spiced red stew served with yellow rice and chutney. The Vierling Saloon is open daily except Sunday from 7:00 A.M. to 9:30 P.M. Dinner is served after 4:00 P.M., and prices range from $8.00 to $12.00.

For an excellent view of all of Marquette, head north of town on County Road 550 for a few miles and turn into the dirt parking lot marked by the large Sugar Loaf sign. This is the start of the ◆ **Sugar Loaf Recreation Trail,** a wide and easy path that winds 0.6 mile up the peak of the same name. You actually climb 315 feet through forest and over granite ridges by a series of steps until you reach the rocky knob marked by a stone monument. The view is spectacular on a clear day, a 360-degree panorama that includes the city, Lake Superior, the rough coastline, and the many islands that lie offshore.

By continuing north on County Road 550 for another 26 miles, you reach its end in the small village of Big Bay on the shores of Lake Independence. Big Bay is best known as a place where scenes for the film *Anatomy of a Murder,* starring Jimmy Stewart and Lee Remick, were shot. The story is true, though the murder really took place at Lumberjack Tavern, a classic north woods bar that was used for one scene in the movie. Other footage was taken in the Big Bay Hotel, which is now the ◆ **Thunder Bay Inn.**

The large inn was built in 1911 as a company store and warehouse and then turned into a hotel. In 1943, Henry Ford purchased it along with the mill at the north end of the lake to produce the wooden parts for his cars. The industrialist extensively remodeled the hotel and reshaped the landscape in front of it. So obsessed was Ford with being able to see his factory from his hotel that he had the town's railroad depot moved and County Road 550 re-routed. It was in 1958, under different owners, that several short scenes of the famous murder mystery were filmed in the hotel's lobby, dining room, and bedrooms upstairs. Eventually the facility was abandoned and sat empty for ten years.

In 1985 Darryl Small bought the hotel and opened the first of twelve rooms two years later. Today the large inn is an interesting place to stay or have dinner. All the rooms have been renovated (you can stay in Ford's Room). Guests begin their day with coffee and rolls served on the second-floor balcony that is furnished with wicker and overlooks the lake and, yes, Ford's old factory. Room rates for double occupancy range from $45 to $55. For reservations call (906–345–9977) or write Thunder Bay Inn, P.O. Box 286, Big Bay 49808.

Another equally interesting place to stay in the area is the ❖ **Big Bay Point Lighthouse,** the secluded retreat located 3.5 miles north of town on Lighthouse Road. The light at Big Bay was built and put into service in 1896 and included a two-story, red brick dwelling with eighteen rooms. The house was divided in half, with the lightkeeper residing in one half and his assistant in the other. The U.S. Coast Guard automated the light in 1941 and then sold it in 1961 after building a new steel tower nearby.

In 1986 the lighthouse became a unique bed and breakfast offering guests the rare opportunity to stay overnight in one of its six bedrooms. The lights stand high above Lake Superior on a rocky point in the middle of forty wooded acres that include 2 miles of trails. You can climb the narrow staircase to the top of the tower for a splendid view of the area, catching a sunrise over Lake Superior at daybreak, a sunset over the Huron Mountains at dusk, or possibly the Northern Lights at night. The interior has been completely renovated and refinished, showing its natural wood and brick, and the various rooms include a delightful sauna.

149

The lighthouse (906–345–9957) is open year-round, with special rates for the off-season, weekdays, and package stays. The basic rate for the summer ranges from $75 to $165 for rooms that sleep from two to four people. For reservations write Lighthouse, 3 Lighthouse Road, Big Bay 49808.

The railroad depot Henry Ford moved in Big Bay is yet another addition to the unusual lodgings found in this small town, thanks to Charlie Drury. After salvaging the depot in 1988 (it had been abandoned for seven years) Drury is now offering history, natural beauty, and a comfortable bed at the ◈ **Big Bay Depot.**

At night, he'll heat up the hot tub on the back deck, and if it's late spring or early summer, guests often enjoy a show of the northern lights right from the oversized tub.

The depot has five large rooms available, featuring private baths, kitchens, and sitting areas. Best of all, every room on the second floor leads out to another deck with a panorama of the lake, anglers jigging for perch, and Ford's old mill.

From Marquette, head north on County Road 550 for 25 miles to Big Bay. The driveway to Big Bay Depot (906–345–9350) is across CR–550 from the Lumberjack Tavern. Rooms are $40 to $50 a night.

The newest Michigan Historical Museum is tucked away in the woods near Negaunee and is probably passed up by many visitors. That's a shame ◈ **Michigan Iron Industry Museum** is an interesting stop that allows you to leisurely explore the history of the Upper Peninsula's iron industry. The museum lies in the forested ravines of the Marquette Iron Range and overlooks Carp River, where the first iron forge in the Lake Superior region was built in 1848. The U.P.'s iron deposits had been discovered four years earlier when William Burt, leader of a U.S. Survey party near the area, noticed the magnetic needle of his compass jumping wildly about. He instructed his men to search the ground, and they immediately turned up outcrops of almost pure iron among the roots of pine trees. The iron era of the U.P. had begun, and in 1846 Jackson Mine, the first operation in the U.P., was opened near Negaunee.

The museum, dedicated in May 1987, does an excellent job of leading you through the history of iron, from its beginnings to its most robust era to the decline of the industry in the 1960s. Inside there are several levels of displays, a reconstructed mine shaft to walk through, and an auditorium that presents a short introductory program. Outside are more artifacts, including a mine locomotive, and trails lead to the old forge site on Carp River. The museum is reached from US–41 by turning onto County Road 492 about 3 miles east of Negaunee and is open daily from 9:30 A.M. until 4:30 P.M. from mid-May until mid-October. Admission is free.

BARAGA COUNTY

Most roadside rest areas in the Upper Peninsula consist of little more than picnic tables, a pair of pit toilets, and a hand pump for water. Then there is one on US–41, 8 miles south of L'Anse. It consists of picnic tables, a pair of pit toilets, a hand pump for water, *and* one of the most beautiful canyons in Michigan. The state's department of transportation maintains the tables and the toilets, but it was forestry students from Michigan Technological University who constructed the wooden boardwalks and observation platforms that make ◈ **Canyon Falls and Gorge** such a pleasant stop.

From the large display map in the rest area, the path departs into the woods, crosses a bridge over Bacco Stream, and within a half mile comes to the impressive Canyon Falls formed by the Sturgeon River. The falls mark the beginning of the canyon by thundering over a rock ledge to the river 30 feet below. Handrails have been erected at this point, and you can lean over the top of the cascade to listen to its roar or to feel the mist the falling water creates.

At this point there is a TRAIL ENDS sign, but the best part of the area, the gorge itself, can only be seen by following the original path, which snakes around a huge rock face. This path hugs the half-mile-long canyon and allows you to view the Sturgeon River, a stretch of roiling white water that rushes sheer rock walls 50 feet in height. All visitors, especially families with young children, should be extremely careful if they choose to continue to the end of the old trail, a one-way mile-long hike. The original log handrails are still up, but they're flimsy and weak in places, and after they end there is nothing between you and the sharp edge of the gorge.

To reach the roof of the state, you have to find ◆**Mount Arvon** in the Upper Peninsula, which at 1,979 feet is 21 feet short of being a true "mountain" but still the highest point in Michigan. The outing involves following unmarked logging roads in a remote section of Baraga County and hoping you can find your way back. Once on top there is no majestic view, just a yellow box in a forest with a register book inside.

But enough people undertake this adventure that the Baraga County Tourism and Recreation Association (906–524–7444) publishes a set of detailed directions to the high point. The association visitor's center is right off US–41 as you enter L'Anse from the east. It has irregular hours.

Although serious research has never been done, many say the largest and best sweet rolls in the state are found at ◆**Hilltop Restaurant,** on US–41 just south of L'Anse. One roll is an ample breakfast for most people since it measures more than 5 inches across and 3 inches thick and arrives filled with cinnamon and dripping in glaze. The restaurant is operated by Judy Jaeger and Vivian Delene, but its sweet-roll fame was already established when they purchased the business in 1975. On a good weekend they will serve more than a thousand. The eatery also has other items on its menu (including good pasties), but who has room for anything else after devouring its sticky specialty with a cup of fresh-brewed coffee? The Hilltop is open from 6:00 A.M. to 8:00 P.M. daily.

One of Baraga County's most interesting attractions is the ◆**Hanka Homestead,** a "living outdoor museum" where visitors learn about and see the lifestyle of the early Finnish farmers who immigrated to what was then a remote and isolated region of the state. The farm dates back to 1896, when the Hanka family applied for a homestead on two forty-acre parcels along the military road to Fort Wilkins at the tip of the Keweenaw Peninsula. The first thing Herman Hanka built was an 18-by-24-foot log house. But he was Finnish, so the second thing he constructed was his *savu,* or smoke sauna. Eventually he added barns, a self-cooling milk house that straddles a small spring, a horse stable, a blacksmith shop, and a granary.

The amazing part about the farm is that it's never been wired for electricity, even though the youngest son, Jalmer Hanka, lived there until 1966. It was added to the National Register of Historic Places in 1984 and opened to the public the next year. Today there are ten buildings and a root cellar to explore, each filled with the Hanka possessions. From US–41 in L'Anse, head north toward Houghton, and in 12 miles turn west on Arnheim Road. Follow the small museum signs. If you pass Otter Lake, you've gone too far west. The Homestead (906–353–7116) is open Saturday and Sunday from noon to 5:00 P.M. May through fall colors in October. There is a small admission fee.

HOUGHTON COUNTY

One of the most spectacular areas of the U.P.'s interior is relatively unknown to travelers who are hesitant to leave paved roads. The ❖ **Sturgeon River Gorge Area** is located just inside Houghton County along its border with Baraga County south of M–38. The wilderness area includes the gorge cut by the Sturgeon River, which in some places is more than 400 feet deep, making it the largest and deepest in the Great Lakes states. For the best view of it, follow M–38 west of Baraga and turn south onto Prickett Dam Road (also called Forest Road 193), marked by a national forest sign. Within 11 miles the road merges into Sturgeon Gorge Road (Forest Road 191), and a few hundred yards to the right there is a sharp 90-degree curve. At this bend an extremely rough jeep trail leads west to the edge of the gorge. It is best to walk the quarter mile that ends at one of the most beautiful panoramas in the U.P. You see the deep gorge below and miles of forested ridges and hills to the west.

Before reaching Sturgeon Gorge Road, you will pass a directional sign for ❖ **Silver Mountain.** Located on the edge of the Sturgeon River Gorge Wilderness in Houghton County, Silver Mountain is a 1,312-foot peak, at one time the site of a fire tower. At a small parking lot, you'll find a long stairway, long as in 250 steps, but once on top you'll see the foundation of the old fire tower, two USGS markers, and a view that includes miles of the rugged Sturgeon River Gorge Wilderness.

In nearby Lake Linden, right downtown on Calumet Avenue, is ❖ **Lindell's Chocolate Shop.** Joseph Bosch had the building erected in 1893 for his Bosch Brewing Company, but in 1918 it was refurbished with wooden ceiling fans, twenty high-backed oak booths, a nickelodeon, leaded-glass windows, and a 6-foot-long marble food preparation table that took four people to lift. It became the Chocolate Shop, and though the entire building was moved down the street in 1928, little of the interior has changed since then.

The menu has, however, as the shop no longer makes candy but specializes in homemade ice cream. Richard and Francis Grunow took over the business in 1977 and still use the 1943 ice-cream maker that is proudly displayed in the shop's front window. You can arise at 4:00 A.M. any day and watch Grunow make the ice cream, or come by at a more reasonable hour and taste one of the four or five flavors he turns out. Lindell's Chocolate Shop (906–296–0793) is also a restaurant and bar with a full menu, but unquestionably it is the ice cream and the malts, milk shakes, sundaes, and banana splits that are its most popular items. The shop is open Monday through Thursday and Saturday from 7:00 A.M. until 7:00 P.M. and on Friday from 7:00 A.M. to 8:30 P.M.; it is closed on Sunday.

KEWEENAW COUNTY

Under the forceful will of President Andrew Jackson, Michigan became a state in 1837, when it grudgingly accepted the entire U.P. in exchange for surrendering Toledo to Ohio. In only six years, this "worthless wilderness" became a land of incredible wealth after Douglas Houghton, the first state geologist, explored the Keweenaw Peninsula and reported finding chunks of pure copper. Miners began arriving by 1841, and within two years there was a lively copper rush to this small section of the U.P., forcing the U.S. Army to build Fort Wilkins in Copper Harbor (today a state historical park) to maintain law and order. As in all stampedes for a precious metal, many mines quickly died, and thousands went home disillusioned and broke. Nevertheless, substantial lodes of copper were uncovered, and by the 1860s this area was producing 15 million pounds annually or almost 90 percent of the national total. Two of the most profitable mines were Calumet and Hecla, and near them sprang up the town of Red Jacket. Later renamed Calumet, this city of 66,000 in 1898 had wealth, importance (it was being considered as a new site for the state capital), and a peculiar problem.

Due to large contributions to the city budget from the mines, the council found itself with a surplus of funds. Already the community had paved streets, electric lights, and telephones, so the town decided to build an opera house, the grandest theater in the Midwest, one that would rival the stages on the East Coast. The ◆ **Calumet Opera House** was built on the corner of Sixth and Elm streets in 1899, and no expense was spared. It was designed in an Italian Renaissance style and inside featured two balconies, private viewing chambers along the walls, and rococo plaster ornamentation of gilt, cream, and crimson. The acoustics were nearly perfect: An actor could whisper on the stage and be heard in the last row of the top balcony.

On March 20, 1900, the first performance was given to a packed house of 1,100 and was described by the *Copper Country Evening News* as "the greatest social event ever known in the copperdome's metropolis." A string of legendary performers arrived at the famed opera house, including John Philip Sousa, Sarah Bernhardt, Douglas Fairbanks, and Lillian Russell. Eventually the theater, like the town, fell upon hard times. The local mines, the last to operate in the Keweenaw Peninsula, were closed for good due to a labor strike in 1968; by then Calumet's population had dwindled to 1,000.

The mines are still closed, but the opera house has since reopened. Declared a National Historic Site in 1974, it was fully restored, and its opulence can be viewed on a guided tour from mid-June to mid-October. Tours are offered daily from 10:00 A.M. to 4:00 P.M., and it's $3.00 for a peek into Calumet's past. It has also returned to live theater after a stint with the motion pictures of the 1920s and 1930s; major performances are scheduled from March through October. Call for information (906–337–2610).

At one time or another in the late 1800s, there were fourteen active copper mines in the Keweenaw Peninsula, and today a number of them have been preserved, offering a glimpse of the underground world of the miners. The least promoted but perhaps the most intriguing is ◆ **Delaware Mine** on US–41 between Calumet and Copper Harbor. To reach it you pass through Delaware, a ghost town of a half dozen abandoned buildings and a sobering reminder that when the copper ran out, so did the lifeblood for boomtowns throughout the peninsula. Interest in the copper at Delaware began in 1845 and

155

Calumet Opera House

involved one early investor by the name of Horace Greeley. The famous newspaper editor actually made a trip to the Keweenaw Peninsula but never traveled much farther than Eagle River. A mining company was organized in 1848, and actual mining began the following year. From 1849 to 1851 the mine produced 522,541 pounds of copper, but the Northwest Copper Mining Company lost almost $100,000 on the operation. The mine was sold again and again to new investors, with one company building a huge hoist house in 1870 to pull the cars out of the deep shafts that were being dug. Despite all efforts, the Delaware never really turned a profit, and the shafts were sealed for good in 1887. The town of Delaware, which in 1879 had 300 residents, also disappeared.

Now a tourist attraction, the Delaware is the only mine you can explore on your own. You begin by donning a hardhat and descending a 100-foot staircase through shaft Number 1 into the first level. The top level is 900 feet of tunnel from which other passages, shafts, and a huge cavern can be viewed. Nine other levels extend 1,400 feet below it, but underground streams have long since flooded all but the first. There is still plenty of copper lying around in this level, and in the information center visitors are told how to recognize and search for it in the mine. They are also given tips afterward on cleaning any metal they find.

You can explore the remains of the hoist house above ground and get a good overview of the ghost town from the parking lot. Delaware Mine (906–289–4688) is open from Memorial Day until mid-October from 10:00 A.M. until 6:00 P.M. daily. There is an admission fee.

The men who actually worked the mines were often immigrants from the Cornwall area of England or from Finland or Norway, and they brought to Copper Country their strong ethnic heritages. Traces of that heritage can be seen in the Cornish pasties that are sold throughout the U.P. and in the popularity of Finnish saunas. For years the sauna took the place of bathtubs and showers in homes, as early settlers would build their sauna huts first and worry about their cabins later. A good sauna begins with a shower to open up the pores of the skin, followed by a stay in a cedar-paneled room where a small pile of rocks is heated. As water is tossed on the rocks, a dry heat emerges that makes the body perspire profusely, flushing out dirt

157

and grime from the skin. The temperature ranges from 160 to 180 degrees, and the old miners used wicker sticks to beat their backs to get the blood moving. The entire ordeal is ended with a cold shower to close the pores.

In Copper Harbor, you can experience this Finnish ritual at ◆ **Brockway Sauna,** operated by Minnetonka Resort in the heart of town on US–41. The public sauna is across the street from the resort and consists of four private suites. Each one is completely paneled in cedar and features a dressing area, shower, and sauna that will seat four to six people. The building is not that far from the shores of Lake Superior, and occasionally a local person will finish the sauna with a mad dash into the chilly lake, a tradition most visitors pass up.

The Brockway Sauna (906–289–4449) is open daily May 15 to October 15 from 1:00 until 10:00 P.M. The price includes use of a room, towel, soap, and a wicker stick if you request it.

The Copper Rush of the Keweenaw Peninsula began in 1843, and Copper Harbor quickly became the center of exploration parties, newly formed mining companies, and a "rough population of enterprising prospectors, miners, and speculators." Due to the seedy nature of the miners and the constant threat of Chippewa tribes wanting to reclaim their lost land, Secretary of War William Wilkins dispatched two companies of infantry to the remote region of Michigan. They arrived in late May of 1844, and by November ◆ **Fort Wilkins** was built.

The threat of Indian hostilities never materialized, and troops discovered the Upper Peninsula winters were long and cold. Isolated from the rest of the world with little more than duty and drill to occupy their time, the garrison of 105 men ran into problems of boredom, low morale, and illegal whiskey. The following year half of the troops were transferred to Texas in preparation for the Mexican War, and in 1846, less than two years after it was built, Fort Wilkins was abandoned. In 1921 Fort Wilkins was recognized as a historic landmark by the state, and in 1923 it was designated a state park. Today the structure is noted for being one of the few surviving wooden forts east of the Mississippi River.

Although the fort was insignificant militarily, it's an outstanding example of a mid-nineteenth-century frontier outpost, as twelve of its sixteen buildings are from the original structure. You can wander through the fort year-round, even ski through it in the winter, but the buildings are open mid-May through mid-October. Ranging from kitchen and mess room to the bakery, company barracks, and hospital, many contain restored furnishings and artifacts depicting the rough life troops endured here. From mid-June to Labor Day, interpreters in period dress give tours daily from 10:00 A.M. until 4:30 P.M., adding a touch of realism to the fort.

The main entrance to the park and the fort is a mile east of Copper Harbor on US–41. For more information on Fort Wilkins or on camping in the state park, call (906) 289–4215.

Keweenaw is the smallest county in the U.P., but it has more than its share of scenic drives, where every curve reveals another striking view. The most famous is the Brockway Mountain Drive, a 10-mile stretch to Copper Harbor that is the highest above-sea-level drive between the Rockies and Alleghenies. Less traveled but almost as scenic in its own way is the ◆**Sand Dune Drive** between Eagle River and Eagle Harbor. From Eagle River this portion of M–26 heads west along the Lake Superior shoreline, climbing high above the water along sandy bluffs. The road provides sweeping views of the Great Lake on the horizon and the sandy shoreline below, and the best turnoff looms above Great Sand Bay. The road returns to the lake level at Cat Harbor, a delightful beach for sunning and swimming if you can handle Superior's chilly waters, and then swings through Eagle Harbor, passing the picturesque **Eagle Harbor Lightstation,** which is now a museum open to the public.

From Eagle Harbor, M–26 continues east, first passing the junction to Brockway Mountain Drive and then returning to the edge of Lake Superior, whose shoreline becomes a rugged mass of red sandstone, gracefully carved by the pounding waves. Along this segment you will pass Devil's Wash Tub, a huge depression in the shoreline that echoes the waves crashing in and out of it.

ONTONAGON COUNTY

Three miles west of Silver City is ◆**Porcupine Mountains Wilderness State Park,** a preserve of 58,000 acres of primitive forests, secluded lakes, and the rugged "Porkies." For most visitors, this state park is a quick drive to the end of M–107, where they follow a short wooded path to the Escarpment, which overlooks Lake of the Clouds, a watery gem in between the peaks and ridges of the mountains. Those willing to don a pair of hiking boots can enjoy some of the most unusual accommodations found in the U.P. with a night in one of the park's rustic cabins.

Within the Porkies is a trail network of more than 85 miles, and scattered along the footpaths are sixteen wilderness cabins, each located in a scenic setting along a stream, lake, or on the shoreline of Lake Superior. You can reach them only on foot, and some are an all-day hike, while others lie only thirty or forty minutes from the nearest parking lot. The cabins have no electricity, running water, or toilets that flush. Modern conveniences are replaced by candles, wood stove, and an outhouse up the hill—ideal for anybody who wants to spend a night in the woods without having to "rough it" in a tent, sleeping on the ground.

Cabins provide bunks, mattresses, cooking utensils, and in the case of those on an inland lake, a small rowboat. You must provide sleeping bag, clothing, and food. The park rents the cabins, which hold from four to eight people, from April through November at $30 per night. Stop at the park visitor's center just off M–107 (open daily from 10:00 A.M. until 6:00 P.M.) for maps and a list of open cabins. Call (906) 885–5275 or write ahead of time for information and a cabin reservation to Porcupine Mountains Wilderness State Park, 412 South Boundary Road, Ontonagon 49953.

Thanks to a rich history of loggers and miners, Michigan is blessed (cursed?) with a scattering of ghost towns throughout the state. Fayette is the most famous and most visited, but ◆**Old Victoria** can be an equally interesting stop. The Ontonagon County town was originally named Cushin and established in 1849 after the discovery of an ancient miner's pit that still contained a mass of copper. In 1858, a new group of investors came in, renamed the mine Victoria, and the company town grew to more than 2,000 residents.

Victoria became a ghost town when the copper ran out. Most of the buildings date back to the late nineteenth century. There are classic hand-hewed log cabins, ruins of a rock house, and mining equipment lying all over the place. Old Victoria is located 4 miles west of Rockland in Ontonagon County with an entrance road that is clearly posted on US–45. Historical tours are given Memorial Day through fall colors in October daily from 11:00 A.M. to 5:30 P.M.

GOGEBIC COUNTY

Waterfalls of every type and description are the gems of the Upper Peninsula, and there are more than 150 of them scattered across this region of Michigan. For example, ◆ **Black River Harbor Drive** (also known as Black River Road and County Road 513) in Gogebic County is virtually a parkway of white-water splendor. The 15-mile road departs from Bessemer on US–2 and enters Ottawa National Forest, ending at scenic Black River Recreation Area on Lake Superior. Heading north you first pass **Copper Peak Ski Flying Hill,** the largest artificial ski slide in the world and the site of 500-foot jumps during the winter. In the summer visitors take the chairlift and elevator to the top for a view of three states and Canada.

From Copper Peak, Black River Road enters the heart of the national forest and winds near five waterfalls, each lying at the end of a trail from a marked turnoff. Gorge and Potawatomi falls are among the most spectacular and easiest to reach. The two falls are within 800 feet of each other and only a five-minute walk from the parking lot. Potawatomi is the largest, with a 130-foot-wide cascade that drops 30 feet into the Black River. Gorge, smaller with a 24-foot drop, is encased in a steep and narrow red rock canyon—a spectacular setting. A well-marked path with stairs and observation decks leads you past both falls.

At the end of the road you can camp at Black River Harbor Recreation Area, or those who desire a little more luxury can rent a log cabin at ◆ **Bear Track Inn** nearby. The small resort has been around since the 1930s, when it catered to lumbermen and commercial fishermen. Its name came from a hungry bear who wandered in one night when they were building the main cabin and walked in the wet cement of the front steps. The name stuck, and the track can still be seen today. The inn has only three cabins for rent, but two are authentic log structures, and all three feature natural wood interior, wood stoves and stone fireplaces, and kitchen facilities. The large cabin can sleep ten, the others hold four people each, and during the summer the rates range from $45 to $58 per night for double occupancy. For reservations call the inn at (906) 932–2144 or write Bear Track Inn, 15325 Black River Road, Ironwood 49938.

IRON COUNTY

Perhaps the U.P.'s largest and least-known historical complex is ❖ **Iron County Museum,** located in the village of Caspian on County Road 424, 2 miles south of US–2 at Iron River. The grounds include almost twenty buildings, many a century old, in a Greenfield Village–like setting that lacks some of the polish of the famous Dearborn attraction but is no less interesting. The park occupies the site of the Caspian Iron Mine, and the head frame that hoisted cars out of the mine in the 1920s still towers over the complex. The main museum is the former engine house, which has been considerably enlarged and today is a maze of displays and three-dimensional exhibits. The favorite is the iron ore mining model that, for a nickel, will automatically run through the process of the rocks being rinsed from the mine and loaded into railroad cars above ground. Other interesting exhibits are the renovated saloon, blacksmith shop, schoolroom, and a hand-carved model of a logging camp that fills an 80-foot display case with hundreds of figures and pieces.

Outside you can wander through one historic building after another: a logging camp bunkhouse with a table set for supper and mackinaw shirts (made of a heavy plaid wool) still hanging up near the door, a barn filled with plows and threshers of the 1800s, a completely furnished homesteaders' cabin, and many other exhibits. You could easily spend an entire day exploring this fascinating folk-life complex. Iron County Museum (906–265–2617) is open mid-May to October from 9:00 A.M. to 5:00 P.M. Monday through Saturday and 1:00 to 5:00 P.M. Sunday. There is a small admission fee.

DICKINSON COUNTY

As in the copper fields, many workers in iron mines were immigrants from Europe. In Iron Mountain, many Italians came to work the Chapin Mine, which was discovered in 1879 and went on to become the second-leading ore producer in the U.P.

You can learn about the miners' life and work at the Menominee Range Historical Museum and see the huge water pump that was built for the exceptionally wet mine at the Cornish Pump and Mining Museum. Or you can enjoy a lively night and a delicious Italian dinner in the old neighborhood.

◆ **The Stables,** a restaurant on Fourth Avenue off US–2, is located in the middle of Iron Mountain's eighteen-block Italian neighborhood. The building was constructed in 1897 to serve as a local pub until Prohibition changed the business into Pietrantonio & Sons Fancy Groceries. Once Prohibition ended, it quickly returned to serving beer; some doubt that it ever stopped. In 1980, Butch Hoyum took over the dilapidated bar, restored its historic decor, and turned it into a fine Italian restaurant while retaining its ethnic quality and the friendliness found in all good neighborhood pubs. He understood what it took because his mother was Italian— "the only reason they accept me around here."

As expected, there is also excellent homemade Italian cuisine including polenta, gnocchi, and ravioli, or you can enjoy a draft beer at what Hoyum claims is the second-oldest bar in the U.P. (Only Shute's in Calumet is older.) Dinner is priced from $6.00 to $12.00 for pasta; prices are higher for other entrees. The Stables (906–774–0890) is open from 11:00 A.M. until 9:00 P.M. Monday through Saturday, and 12:30 to 9:00 P.M. on Sunday. Dinner reservations are recommended.

The Menominee River forms almost half of the border between Wisconsin and Michigan's Upper Peninsula, beginning west of Iron Mountain and extending to its mouth on Green Bay. Two miles south of Norway the river flows through ◆ **Piers Gorge,** a white-water area of large falls, holes, and swirls as the river tumbles through a scenic forested canyon. The gorge picked up its name in the 1840s when loggers built piers along this section of the river in an attempt to slow down the current and prevent logs from jamming and splitting on the jagged rocks. You can view this spectacular stretch of wild water by heading south of Norway on US–8; just before its bridge across the Menominee, turn left onto Piers Gorge Road. The paved road quickly turns into a dirt one, and then after 0.6 mile it ends at a footpath. A hike of 0.8 mile brings you to a series of viewing points above the falls.

During the summer you can also experience the gorge and what many rafters call the "Midwest's premier white-water river"

IXL Office Museum

through Argosy Rafting Adventures Inc. The company offers a three-hour raft trip that takes you through Piers Gorge and over its falls. On Saturday and Sunday, the rafters meet nearby at various times and then proceed to the river with their large inflated rafts. It's a wild ride, one that will leave you soaking wet but exhilarated. The company provides the rafts, guides, helmets, life jackets, and a paddle for each passenger.

Argosy Rafting Adventures (715–251–3886) is based in Wisconsin. The cost for the raft trips, which also can be set up during the week by advance reservation, is around $30 per person.

MENOMINEE COUNTY

One of the products of Michigan's white pine era was hardwood floors by the IXL Company of Hermansville. Established by C. J. Meyer in the 1870s as part of his Wisconsin Land and Lumber Company, IXL became world-renowned for its floors after machines were invented in Hermansville that could precision-manufacture tongue-and-groove hardwood flooring in one operation. By the early 1900s it was the largest such plant in the country, and IXL flooring could be seen (and walked on) in the main lodge at Yellowstone National Park and the Mormon Temple in Salt Lake City.

In 1881 Meyer erected a huge office building to manage his sprawling lumber operation, and today it's one of the most intriguing museums in the Upper Peninsula. The ◆ **IXL Office Museum** is literally a step into a nineteenth-century business office. On the first floor visitors wander through the payroll and accounting departments as well as the private offices of the company executives. All are fully furnished and appear as if the workers had just stepped out for lunch. In one room there are dictaphones, mimeographs, typewriters, and other machines complete with instruction booklets, while across the hall beautiful rolltop desks and an ornate walk-in vault can be seen. On the second floor several rooms are devoted to the machinery and equipment used in the flooring industry, and on the third floor visitors can still flip through original payroll records and see what a worker earned each week (along with deductions) in the 1890s.

The museum is located in the heart of Hermansville, a small town on US–2, 26 miles west of Escanaba and 30 miles east of Iron Mountain. The museum (906–498–2498) is open June through Labor Day from 12:30 to 4:00 P.M. daily. There is a small admission fee.

Appendix

The following are state and regional tourist offices, which can provide the most up-to-date information on accommodations, restaurants, and attractions in the areas they represent:

Michigan Travel Bureau
P.O. Box 30226
Lansing, MI 48909
800–543–2937

West Michigan Tourist Association
136 Fulton Street, East
Grand Rapids, MI 49503
616–456–8557

Upper Peninsula Travel and Recreation Association
618 Stephenson Avenue
P.O. Box 400
Iron Mountain, MI 49801
906–774–5480

INDEX

Entries for Museums and Park and Natural Areas appear in the special indexes beginning on page 172.

SPECIAL INDEXES

ABOUT THE AUTHOR

Jim DuFresne is a Detroit-based travel and outdoor writer whose syndiated columns, "Travels in Michigan" and "Kidventures," appear in daily newspapers across the state. Formerly a sports and outdoors editor for the Juneau Empire in Alaska, DuFresne published his first travel book, *Tramping in New Zealand,* in 1982. His other books include *Isle Royale National Park; Voyageurs National Park; Alaska: A Travel Survival Kit; Glacier Bay National Park: A Backcountry Guide to the Glaciers and Beyond; Michigan State Parks;* and *Micigan's Best Outdoor Adventures with Children.*

UNITED STATES TRAVEL
Off the Beaten Path™ Series

Visit fascinating and unusual places with these outstanding tour guides available now in your local bookstore. With the following new additions to this award-winning series adventurous travelers can now go off the beaten path in every American state! Please check your local bookstore for fine Globe Pequot Press titles, which include:

The Dakotas $10.95
A striking diversity of unusual adventures from the Badlands to Hot Springs

Utah $10.95
From camping adventures to Indian village sites in a state full of natural wonders

Mississippi $10.95
Lovely locales and historical outposts in a beautiful and interesting state

Oklahoma $10.95
The best places to take advantage of Oklahoma's striking natural beauty

Nevada $10.95
Great cities, parks and beyond in a state that offers far more than most visitors see.

AND NOW,
FOR THE FIRST TIME,
OFF THE BEATEN PATH™
IS GOING TO CANADA!!

**The Maritime Provinces
                          $10.95**
The first Off the Beaten Path™ guide to cross the border! Explore the lesser-known delights of Canada's Atlantic Coast provinces.

Available from your bookstore or directly from the publisher. For a free catalogue or to place an order, call toll-free 24 hours a day (1-800-243-0495), or write to The Globe Pequot Press, P.O. Box 833, Old Saybrook, Connecticut 06475-0833.